REAL ESTATE
IS NOT
ROCKET SCIENCE

OTHER BOOKS BY STEVE SHULL

The Full Fee Agent: How to Stack the Odds in Your Favor as a Real Estate Professional

The Real Estate Team Playbook: Work Smarter. Profit More. Get Your Life Back.

STEVE SHULL

REAL ESTATE

IS NOT

ROCKET
SCIENCE

*The Six Core Building Blocks
to Succeed In Any Market*

Ballast Books, LLC
www.ballastbooks.com

ISBN: 978-1-962202-05-3

Printed in the United States of America

Published by Ballast Books
www.ballastbooks.com

For more information, bulk orders, appearances, or speaking requests,
please email: info@ballastbooks.com

*This book is dedicated to every real estate professional
I have worked with—past, present, and future.
Your success is my success.
This book is a tribute to your dedication, grit, and resilience.
May it inspire and empower you to reach new heights.
Always remember that real estate is a blue sky business,
and it's not rocket science.*

CONTENTS

FOREWORD BY **ROB GIEM**

I have worked with Steve Shull for over twenty-five years. In that time, my career went from the ordinary to the extraordinary. Agents and clients frequently ask me how I got to where I am today, and I tell them that the tools I was given in my private coaching sessions with Steve transformed my business—because they did. Those tools changed how I thought about the business, myself, my processes, and how I viewed my potential for success. That last one was the most important because I was the only person limiting my success at the time.

Whatever your personal challenges are, you are looking for the answers. That is how you got here and why you are reading this now. I can tell you this book clearly sets out a path for how to radically alter your business for the better. In concise language, and with a clear plan, Steve directs you away from the noise and paints a truthful picture of the business, what to do (and what not to do), and how to get ahead in a logical, methodical, and calculated way. It is precisely this information that has the potential—in the hands of a willing and coachable student—to transform their career. It did for me.

And please don't assume I was destined for my success, because I was not. My first decade in the business was a bust. I was not a diamond in the rough. Rather, I was the person least likely to succeed. I am a dedicated introvert, and I would never be described as a gifted salesperson. Instead, I prefer rational processes and calculable outcomes. There couldn't be a worse personality profile for real estate. So, as you would suspect, success did not come easily for me. It was a hard road from the beginning as I watched people all around me doing all the wrong things. By the time I met Steve, I was worn out, and practically washed out. Worst of all, I had lost faith in the future of my career because I could not see any path forward.

What I learned in my coaching with Steve was the catalyst for the change that took me from being an inconsistent, midlevel producer to being at the top—a place where I have comfortably stayed for over two decades since.

My questions for you are: How open are you to change? How open are you to setting aside the myths of real estate and focusing on the facts? In other words, how coachable are you? If you're ready to learn and change, and you're willing to adapt yourself to a successful mindset coupled with a dependable plan, then the only thing separating you from your next level of success is reading this book and putting it into action. If you are ready, in time you will find your success—and you won't have to waste a decade like I did.

Read. Listen. Learn. Act. That's about all it takes.

From our first day in this business, we watch and absorb what we see around us. With no guides, and no readily available roadmaps to success, we are desperate for information. Over time, what we absorb, good or bad, becomes too much information. Our brains fill up. Not a lot of it makes sense, and it's even harder to sort through it all objectively. Over time, whether we realize it or not, this accumulation of information becomes a quicksand of sorts. It traps you in the same place, making you question your decisions more with every passing day. This ultimately keeps you from moving forward efficiently.

Steve has taken his thirty years of experience coaching thousands of agents across the country and distilled it into a plan we can all use. In reading this book, I was reminded of how he brought me out of that quicksand. For me, this book has brought everything full circle—and again has pulled me forward into another era of new success.

INTRODUCTION

Not long ago, I met a real estate agent who was at the top of her game in every way.

She was making more money than she ever expected, and her business just kept growing. She had the space and flexibility to do all the other things she cared about, like spending quality time with her family and traveling. She felt confident in her planning, decision-making, and execution in every aspect of her business.

In short, real estate had turned out to be everything she had dreamed of. Her life was perfect, and she was loving every minute of it.

Just kidding.

I talk to thousands of real estate agents every year, and that story has never once been true. It *is*, however, what most people imagine will happen when they become real estate agents. That's what attracts people to this business: the promise of earning a six-figure income, being your own boss, and having a flexible schedule.

The dream of what real estate can be is very alluring.

However, those expectations can get crushed very quickly. The new agents I meet usually find themselves working unexpectedly long days to build their client base—not to mention being on call 24/7. They wanted to be their own boss, but it turns out that's a hard job, and they're feeling the anxiety and loneliness of having to make every decision themselves. Every dollar is a battle, and there's never enough. They think, *If only I could sell more, I'd achieve the dream I set out with.*

But the grass is not greener on the other side. Top-producing agents suffer just as much, if not more. After years of pounding the pavement and building their empires from scratch, they're still working twelve-plus-hour days and on call 24/7. They're still bad at being their own boss. They still want more sales. Only now they have more to lose, so their stress levels are even higher. Even worse, they are still giving away their commissions to put deals together.

I've been coaching real estate agents for more than thirty years, so I've seen this over and over and over. Every agent, new or experienced, aspiring or top performer, struggles almost every day.

Virtually everyone responds to this dilemma in the same way: by looking for new ideas. They think some other agent has sourced the "magic pill." *Something* has to be easier, faster, or more effective than what they're doing now. So they try different things—send a mailer, run an ad, up their social media game, buy some leads, revamp their listing presentation—anything that might move the needle.

The problem is, they can't tell what works and what doesn't. So, they just do what feels good or urgent at the moment—which usually means chasing after deals indiscriminately.

It seems logical, but instead of leading to more success, this approach leaves them stuck and frustrated. They're exhausted and perpetually racing to catch up. They're always too busy reacting to the present situation to plan for the future. They feel like the only way to grow their business is to work harder, but they're already maxed out.

Sound familiar?

YOU DON'T NEED A NEW IDEA

It *is* possible to succeed in this business without constant work, stress, and overwhelm, but there are no shortcuts to that outcome. As you'll soon learn, real estate is a blue-sky business, and opportunity is truly everywhere. You just won't get there by looking for shiny new ideas. In over thirty years, I have yet to hear a good new idea in real estate.

At its heart, this is a very simple business.

People complicate it all the time, and usually not with your best interests in mind. All those quick fixes and secret strategies that land in your inbox—*10 Listings in 90 Days! Get Every Buyer to Buy NOW!*—are snake oil. They don't work.

How do I know? Because the moment markets get tough, top agents abandon that nonsense. If it really produced more business, they would do even more of it when times are hard. But they don't. They go back to the basics . . . because that's what produces results.

Those basics are the foundation of your business. You're a real estate agent; you know the importance of a strong foundation for a house. Well, same for your business. Too many agents build theirs on air—on the hope that some new twist can generate instant and lasting results. They ignore the basics and grasp at anything that seems like it can bring in leads instantly.

It doesn't work. Success in this business comes down to mastering those basics. Everything else, especially anything that promises instant gratification, is a waste of time and money. And despite advances in technology, the basics haven't changed. That's why, after thirty years in this business, I'm still coaching people on the same foundational concepts.

But while the fundamentals are simple, executing them consistently is not easy. You must be willing to look inward and become intensely self-aware. You have to unwind a lot of bad habits that have been in place for a really long time. You need an unwavering commitment to show up every day with a growth mindset, do your job (as you will learn in this book), put in your reps, and be accountable to the process.

If you can bring those qualities to the table, I can teach you the rest. In this book, you'll learn three things:

1. **How to be coachable.** Without this, everything else is useless. No amount of guidance will help you if you don't commit to following it.
2. **How to grow a repeat and referral business.** There are just six building blocks to master. As you'll see, how you do business is more important than how much business you do.
3. **How to enjoy every day no matter what.** If you can't do that, what's the point? Don't kid yourself that you'll be happy if or when you achieve some goal—there's always another goal after that to keep your happiness out of reach.

These three skills are all it takes to succeed in real estate without burning out. Mastering them will allow you to do more than just make great money. You'll also be able to enjoy your work and feel valued by your clients. Most importantly, you'll have the free time and peace of mind to actually live your life—not just survive.

I HAVE SOME BAD NEWS

Here's the catch: the fundamentals are things you will *not* want to do.

I didn't make it this way on purpose. The six building blocks you'll learn in this book are the result of constantly refining my coaching process over many years. They just *happen* to be the six things agents hate the most. Funny how that worked out. They'll make you uncomfortable, and most agents let those feelings of discomfort get in the way of doing what needs to be done.

But you don't succeed in life by avoiding the things you don't want to do.

You've probably heard the popular "wisdom" that if you follow your passion, you'll never work a day in your life. Sorry, but that's BS. To be able to follow your passion, you have to do a *lot* of things that feel like work.

I learned this from an early age. I grew up playing sports, and my first career was in pro football as a linebacker for the Miami Dolphins. To succeed in sports, you have to master the fundamentals, and most of that stuff is not fun. It's hard work. In eleven years of playing serious football, there was never a single day that I wanted to go practice . . . but I also never missed a practice just because I didn't want to go.

Why? Because I wanted the result. I wanted to play in the game, do well, and be on a winning team. To have that, I had to do what my coach told me and put in the reps (plus a whole lot more on my own time), even when they were painful, boring, or difficult.

Real estate is no different. If you want to be a top agent, there's a lot of unglamorous work you have to do. There's no getting around it. But if you're willing to do that work, the results can be spectacular.

When I entered the real estate business in 1991, I started at square zero. I was in a new place with no database, no friends, no experience, and no knowledge of the area. It was my third career, after pro football and Wall Street.

Like most new agents, I wanted to make a lot of money quickly without making a big investment. I had heard an interview with two agents who were on track to sell one hundred homes in just their second year. They talked about how the business worked and how they approached it, and everything they said just clicked. It was simple. I understood the basics in about two minutes, and I knew immediately that I could do what it took to be successful.

I started out with a partner who had been in the business for a while already, doing ten to twelve transactions a year. The training we were getting at the time spelled out four different options for generating business: door knocking, calling expired listings, calling for-sale-by-owner listings, and cold calling. I chose the first two.

To be clear, I didn't want to do *any* of those things. I had played in a Super Bowl. I had worked for Salomon Brothers on their Treasury desk doing multimillion-dollar trades. The idea of knocking on doors and calling strangers in Fullerton, California seemed like quite a letdown . Who wants to spend all day bothering people who just want to go about their lives uninterrupted? But those were my options, and I chose the ones that seemed the least awful.

For four or five hours a day, I prospected. I worked up from twenty-five doors a day to two hundred, and I called every single expired listing in my target areas, every day. Same script every time. It wasn't fun, but I knew it was necessary to get the results I wanted. No one was going to outwork me. Through diligent follow-up, some of those contacts became leads, and some of those leads ultimately became clients.

That first year, in the worst market imaginable, my partner and I sold fifty-three homes.

It didn't happen because of raw talent or exclusive insight. It came from consistent execution of the fundamentals.

ARE YOU READY TO BE COACHED?

My early success in real estate quickly transformed into the idea of creating a coaching program for agents. I've always been a coach by nature. All day long, I think about how to do things better and make other people successful.

By now, I've coached more real estate agents one-on-one than anybody in the world. They say it takes 10,000 hours of practice to become an expert, and I've done six times that in coaching new agents, top teams, and everyone in between. Hopefully, you gain a lot of wisdom when you spend 60,000-plus hours doing something you love.

What I've seen is there are a lot of dark alleys you can go down in this business. Even top-selling agents make choices that waste huge amounts of time and money, often without realizing it. That's why, if you ask ten experienced agents for advice, you'll hear ten different things—what worked for each particular agent. Not what has worked for thousands of agents. Not what is most likely to work for you.

You don't have time to explore all those dark alleys and make all those mistakes yourself. Save yourself the pain and accelerate your growth by learning from the many, many agents I've coached before you. I don't pretend to know everything, but in this business, there's very little I haven't seen before. I know what I know and what I don't know, and I know what matters and what doesn't.

All that knowledge is in these pages: a step-by-step playbook to building a thriving real estate business. That includes both the actions you must take every day and the mindset you must develop to execute them consistently.

Part I sets you up for success by addressing the biggest obstacles head-on. In Chapter 1, we'll clear up common misunderstandings about what the real estate business is and how it really works. In Chapter 2, we'll tackle the number one force that undermines you every day: fear. In Chapter 3, you'll learn what it means to be coachable and how that will make or break your business.

In Part II (Chapters 4–9), you'll learn the six building blocks of every real estate business. These are the fundamentals I've been going on about so much:

- **A Mindset of Harmony:** this is the crucial mental shift that makes it possible to stop chasing deals, focus on what works, and enjoy every day.
- **Time Blocking:** time is your most precious asset, and this is how you take control of it.
- **CRM:** this is your most powerful business-building tool—the one that most agents misuse or ignore entirely.
- **Process Management:** this is how you create a great experience for your clients, quality of life for yourself, and scalability for your business.
- **Tactical Empathy:** this is the skill that makes you a trusted advisor to your clients and keeps them coming back to you.
- **Numbers Tracking:** this is how you know what's really happening in your business—not through intuition, but through data.

Part III will help you put all this into practice. In Chapter 10, you'll learn how to become a master of execution—the kind of agent who knows what their job is and just does it. In Chapter 11, you'll learn what all this means for real estate teams, and what a true team really is. In Chapter 12, it all comes together in one choice: the fee you charge. The goal is to become a full fee agent, without constant stress and overwhelm. It's the best outcome not only for you, but for your clients as well.

This book is not about working harder—it's about working smarter and more consciously. That may sound cliché, but it's true. Most agents work very hard at the wrong things and avoid doing the things that get results. They waste time, energy, and money looking for a better way, trying things that don't work. Working smarter and more consciously means cutting that stuff out and focusing on what truly matters. No new ideas—just the fundamentals. It's more uncomfortable at first, but it will get you far better results in far less time.

That discomfort will be a major theme throughout the book. You need to get comfortable being uncomfortable, which might sound painful right now, but don't worry. You'll learn to master this skill and realize the incredible freedom and power it brings.

This book is also not simply about selling more. More is not necessarily better—ask my coaching clients who sell hundreds of millions a year and are still miserable. *How* you achieve more determines whether it is better or not. That's why this book is about process, not goals or results. Your process is the only thing you can control, and if you focus on executing it better and better, the results will follow.

For any of this to work, you must *want* to get better. That's no trivial thing. Everyone "wants" to get better—until they have to put their soul where their mouth is and do what it really takes. Performing at the highest level means committing to making a change, and that commitment is a powerful thing. As noted political and cultural commentator David Brooks said, "The life well lived is a journey from open options to unwavering commitments." To get the results you want in your business, you must commit to doing things differently from the way you've done them in the past.

It won't transform your business instantly—nothing will. Real estate doesn't work that way. There's nothing you can do today that will result in business tomorrow. It takes time and consistent cultivation for the seeds you plant today to bear fruit. But if you're always looking for instant gratification, you'll never do what it takes to build a thriving business. This is a thirty-plus-year career—treat it that way. If you're not willing to do that, reading this book is a waste of your time.

The real question is, how long do you want to keep doing what you've always done if it's not getting you what you want? This is the human predicament: we insist on doing what's familiar over and over, hoping one day it will work, even though it never has before. That's the classic definition of insanity. Until you realize that, you'll stay stuck in this loop and never get anywhere.

Real estate is not rocket science. It's a battle for consistency. You have to learn what your job is and just do it—and this book will teach you how.

PART I:
SOME ESSENTIAL TRUTHS

1: THE NATURE OF REAL ESTATE

Several months ago, I started working with an agent who had gone on 150 listing appointments in the previous year. He was hired 50 percent of the time, which means he got seventy-five listings, and the vast majority of those turned into closed deals. That would be a pretty great year, by most agents' standards.

But I see a problem there: 50 percent. Year after year, with agent after agent, I've tracked this hit rate, and somehow, it always turns out to be something like 50 percent.

If you really get hired based on the quality of your listing presentation, a 50 percent ratio makes no sense. People with great presentation skills should win way more of those appointments, and those who give subpar presentations should win way less. That would be consistent with the 80-20 principle, which says that in most things, 80 percent of the results come from 20 percent of the efforts. In other words, the top presenters should be killing it . . . but they're not.

And therein lies the false premise that drives the entire real estate industry: that you win or lose business based on your presentation (and, to a lesser degree, the commission you charge).

It's simply not true. That ubiquitous 50- percent hit rate isn't telling us that virtually all agents are of about average skill when it comes to listing presentations—that's definitely not the case. It's telling us that fifty-fifty is a flip of the coin.

Here's the truth: You're either the Favorite or the Fool *before* you ever set foot in someone's home. They either intend to do business with you or don't, and that decision is 80 percent made before they meet you. No amount of presentation skill will meaningfully change your hit rate.

If you're skeptical of this, join the club. We'll come back to it again later. The point is that this *one* revelation about the nature of this business radically changes your approach.

Before, your goal was to go on as many listing appointments as possible and knock their socks off with your presentation. But if you accept the premise of the Favorite or the Fool, that no longer makes sense. Now, your goal is to determine whether you are the Favorite or the Fool—and not waste your time on appointments where you were never going to get the listing, no matter how great your presentation is.

This myth about the power of your listing presentation isn't the only misunderstanding that leads agents astray. In this chapter, I'll lay out eight things every agent needs to understand about the nature of this industry. These are the realities, but they're not necessarily obvious. Even when they are, too many agents fail to act accordingly. But not you—at least, not by the end of this chapter.

1. REAL ESTATE IS A BLUE-SKY BUSINESS

Anybody—*anybody*—can become a real estate agent. You can start at ground zero, and there are no limits to your productivity. You don't need a pedigree, money, a network, or a fancy education. You don't need to be familiar with the geographic area. All you have to do is take a few hours of training and pass a fairly simple exam.

The only one who can stop you is you. It's not a cliché—it's the literal truth. Nothing and nobody is going to get in your way. The barrier to entry is that low.

At the same time, there are no guarantees either. No one is going to hand you a starter kit and hold your hand until you find success. You're basically on your own, and while your limitations may be self-imposed, they have very real consequences.

That's why it's so important to recognize the excuses for what they are: internal roadblocks. Here are the most common ones:

"I don't know enough people."

Go out and meet some. Knock on doors, go to meetings and events, talk to people. If you add one new person to your CRM (client relationship management system) every workday, in a year, you'll have at least two hundred. Within three years, you'll have at least five hundred, and you don't need more than that. Of those five hundred plus, about 5 percent will move in a given year, and twenty-five-plus deals a year is great for most agents.

"I don't have money to promote myself."

Neither did I, but there are ways to build your business without money—like knocking on doors and calling expired listings.

"I can't compete against experienced people."

In any market, something like *half* of all deals are done with agents who only do one or two deals a year. Clearly, experience isn't everything. Just ask Jeffrey Saad, one of my longtime coaching clients. When asked about his experience very early on in his career, Jeffrey saw himself as a top performer from day one. "I may be new to real estate," he would say, "but I'm not new to business."

As you'll learn throughout this book, this business is about building trust, not winning a beauty contest based on your past sales figures. But hey, if you're really that worried about being green, join a team. That way, you can borrow someone else's track record from day one.

Every one of these excuses has a simple solution. You can have any excuse you want; just understand that it's an excuse. People succeed in this business from every background imaginable, even if they didn't succeed in other careers. It's a blue-sky business, if you can only get out of your own way.

(That said, the one thing you can't avoid is talking to people. If you don't want to do that, you're going to have a hard time as a real estate agent.)

2. REAL ESTATE IS A RELATIONSHIP BUSINESS

You are not in the business of selling property. You are not in the business of doing deals. You are not in the business of chasing dollars. Again, this is not a glorified beauty pageant—although you wouldn't know it by looking around at all the agents bragging about selling gazillions of dollars in homes and being number one in their market. That noise is irrelevant.

You are in the people business. You are in the relationship business. You are in the business of helping people find their place in the world—find *home*.

This is sacred. There is no other way to explain it.

If you give any consumer a choice to work with someone they know and trust versus a complete stranger who is a beauty pageant winner, who will they choose? The person they trust, almost every single time. That's why so many deals happen with small-time agents. Those clients went with the agent they trusted, because who cares if they're not a big shot?

If you think your job is to sell, you will chase people, persuade them, and push them to do what *you* think is right on *your* time-line because *you* want to close another deal. When your driving purpose is to close deals, the process is inherently about you, not the client. That only serves to alienate people, which is why you find it so hard to convert leads and get repeat and referral business. Everything is a struggle because you're at odds with the natural process of real estate.

That natural process is grounded in relationships and trust. There are no shortcuts to the relationship-building process. Good relationships are hard. They don't happen by accident. They require you to be faithful, empathetic, generous, open, and willing to be part of a larger whole. They require you to surrender your ego, let go of your desires and fears, and accept the person and situation in front of you.

Most of all, they require *time*. Trust is the foundation of every good relationship, and it can only be earned one step at a time. Being a trusted advisor means always putting the client's interests first. It is not about you . . . it's about them.

Most of the industry is still focused on chasing leads, not building relationships. That's why Zillow and all the other lead-generation companies exist. The whole idea is to circumvent the relationship process. If you do that, your connection to the client can't be anything more than transactional, and when you view the client in a transactional way, they view you that way as well. They'll never see you as a trusted advisor or give you repeat and referral business, which is why chasing leads doesn't lead to long-term success. Nothing with a short-term orientation ever does.

Do some people build real estate businesses by collecting massive numbers of low-quality leads and converting 1–3 percent of them into clients? Yes, they do, and on the surface, those businesses may look successful. But I promise you, it takes far more work and leads to an inferior experience for both you and the client, which is why that business model will never allow you to have reliable profits *and* great quality of life at the same time.

3. REAL ESTATE IS A PROGRESSION

Here's the progression I learned on my first day in real estate:

Contacts → leads → appointments → listings → sales

It's a simple funnel. Contacts are people you've talked to. Some of those contacts will be interested in doing business with you, and they'll become leads. Some of those leads will make appointments to learn more. Some of those will sign listing or buyer agreements, and hopefully most of those will lead to closed sales.

Your job is to create contacts by going out and talking to people. The rest flows naturally from there. If you want more sales, start with more contacts.

That fundamental progression is still true, but I've made a few improvements over the years. Here's the first tweak:

**Contacts → leads → appointments → listings → sales →
*repeat & referral***

The first progression focused on prospecting. Here, the focus shifts to generating repeat and referral business from previous clients. Why? Because repeat and referral business is much easier, more efficient, more profitable, and more enjoyable—essentially, better in every way.

Here's the next adjustment:

**Contacts → *connections* → *relationships* → leads →
appointments → listings → sales → repeat & referral**

In the beginning, the idea was to convert contacts to leads . . . but that's impossible. You can't convince someone to buy or sell a house when they weren't already planning to. Contacts become leads when *they're ready*. You don't need to convince them, just build a trusting relationship—as you just learned a moment ago.

That relationship starts with a connection. Making a contact is just talking to someone; making a connection is establishing rapport. Give them a reason to like and trust you, and they'll engage in the ongoing conversation that builds a relationship.

And now, for the final polish:

Contacts → connections → relationships → leads → pre-appointments → listings → sales → repeat & referral

If what I said about the Favorite or the Fool is true (and it is), you need to find out which one you are before you go on an appointment that might take a whole day of your time. So, you do a short video call first to find out where you stand. If you're the Favorite, they'll commit to working with you before you agree to meeting in person and doing all the prep work that entails. If not, they won't, and you don't have to waste your time on an appointment that leads to nothing.

If this sounds crazy to you now, it will all become clear in Chapter 8, where you'll learn about Tactical Empathy. That's the fundamental idea that leads to the Favorite or the Fool as well as several other techniques that will transform the way you interact with clients.

Each of these tweaks seems small, but the difference between where we started and where we ended up is fundamental.

The first progression had a *transactional* orientation. It asked you to sell your value and convince people with facts, logic, and reason. This is at odds with the nature of the real estate business, which, as you now know, is fundamentally a relationship business.

The new progression has a *relational* orientation. It asks you to build on trust, not by convincing but by making people feel understood. That's in alignment with the nature of the business.

4. EVERY DEAL IS A MIRACLE

Noah Lyles is an American track star with two World Championships, an Olympic medal, and an American record in the 200-meter sprint. As he put it, "World records don't get broken when you're ready. They get broken when the day is ready."

There are a lot of things that have to line up perfectly: the weather, the track, the competition, the energy, the crowd, and more. None of that is under his control. The only thing he can control is whether he is ready, and that is just one factor of many. The outcome is mostly out of his hands.

The same is true of real estate. Just because you're ready to sell a home doesn't mean a home is going to sell. If all the other factors don't line up—the buyer, the seller, the financing, the inspection, etc.—it's just not going to happen. The day isn't ready.

If you're like most agents, you've been taught that you have to make sales happen. So when they don't happen, you think something is wrong with you, you're doing something wrong, or you're not doing enough.

That's not true. It just means everything didn't line up.

The idea that if you do X things, you'll always get Y results— that's a false claim. As much as some trainers and speakers want you to believe that the business of real estate is formulaic, it's not. You can't make miracles happen, can you? Well, every real estate deal is a miracle. A thousand little things have to line up for it to happen, and the vast majority of those are outside your control. You can only be ready, and wait patiently for the day to be ready too.

Until you understand this, you will never find happiness or peace in this business. Every time things don't line up, you'll get impatient and start questioning and changing everything you do. You'll stop focusing on the fundamentals and start looking for quick fixes and magic pills. And then when the day *is* ready, you'll be the one who isn't.

5. HOPES AND DREAMS ARE ON THE LINE

Your job as a real estate agent is to sell reality to people whose hopes and dreams are *not* based in reality.

Every seller thinks their house is worth more than it is, it's perfect just the way it is, and everyone will line up to make an offer. They don't understand that getting top dollar for a home takes financial investment, effort, and patience.

Every buyer thinks they can buy the perfect home for half of what it actually costs. They believe that if they haven't seen it yet, they just haven't looked enough. They don't understand that there's no such thing as a perfect home, and pretty costs more.

These hopes and dreams are based on emotion, and you can't overcome emotion with facts, logic, and reason. Getting your clients to accept reality is no easy task—reality doesn't compare to the fantasy world of their hopes and dreams. But until you can guide them to think realistically, they can't move forward.

This is a skill. It takes no skill at all (but lots and lots of work) to show someone dozens of homes, catering to their delusional conviction that the perfect one will come along if they just keep looking. What if you could do things differently so that they're ready to make an offer after a small handful—not dozens—of showings? That's what happens when you learn how to sell reality.

You can't sell reality to your clients unless *you* learn to deal with it first. It's a question of hope versus truth—which currency do you deal in? Which standard do you hold yourself accountable to?

Most agents, like their clients, cling to hope. They *hope* their buyers will stick with them all the way to a closed sale, instead of actually having them sign an agreement. They *hope* they'll get paid something, instead of insisting on charging what they're worth. They keep names in their database and *hope* they'll turn into business, instead of committing to being in a relationship with those people.

This is concrete, not abstract. When you make decisions based on reality and truth, you do different things every day than if you're clinging to hope. You can no longer just do whatever feels good or urgent and hope that your business will somehow magically thrive. You have to elevate your game and focus on doing the *right* things—the six building blocks you'll learn about soon.

The thing about the truth is that it always comes out eventually. The question is whether you want the truth now or later. Hope just kicks the can down the road, moving you further away from what you want in life. That's why this book is about dealing in reality, not fantasy.

As Katie Phang (long-time trial lawyer and host of *The Katie Phang Show* on MSNBC) said, "Sure, as a lawyer, you perfect the art of the spin. But at the end of the day, and no matter how hard you try to make it look nicer or sound better, it's the truth that will either bring victory or a crushing defeat." If it's true for lawyers, it's definitely true for you.

6. EVERY FORCE IMAGINABLE IS CONSPIRING AGAINST YOU

Everyone in this business is trying to make you work harder for less money. Your brokerage, your clients, your competition, the market . . . even your own internal stories.

You need to recognize this, or you'll become a commodity. Commodities are interchangeable; they compete only on price, and it's a race to the bottom. The moment you start competing for business by overpromising results and discounting your commission, you've entered that race. It's unwinnable: there's always another agent who will promise more and charge less.

Don't fight that current. Instead, step out of it.

To help you understand what I mean, here's a parable known as Life in Five Short Chapters:

I. I walk down the street. There is a deep hole in the sidewalk. I fall in. I am lost. I am helpless. It isn't my fault. It takes forever to find a way out.
II. I walk down the same street. There is a deep hole in the sidewalk. I still don't see it. I fall in again. I can't believe I am in the same place. It isn't my fault. It still takes a long time to get out.
III. I walk down the same street. There is a deep hole in the sidewalk. I see it there, but I still fall in. It's a habit. It's my fault. I know where I am. I get out immediately.
IV. I walk down the same street. There is a deep hole in the sidewalk. I walk around it.
V. I walk down a different street.

Most agents are stuck in Chapter II. Over and over again, they allow themselves to become a commodity by walking down the street of value selling and falling into the hole of discounting their fee. They don't even realize their mistake; most will defend their decision to discount. They'll say they have to do it because everyone else does, and something is better than nothing—both of which are patently untrue.

The top performers are the guiltiest. In real estate, the higher the price point, the steeper the discount. It makes no sense. In what other business do the best charge the least? And if you only get business by cutting discounts, you're a commodity, not a top performer. Tom Brady didn't give his money away to get a touchdown—that option doesn't exist in football. In your own business, just because giving your money away is an option doesn't mean you should. In doing so, you're shortchanging both you and your clients.

This book is meant to elevate your level of professionalism, and that means charging a full fee. This point will be repeated over and over again throughout these pages. People think it's impossible, but it's not. You don't have to be a commodity to succeed. You don't have to give your money away or be a doormat or work with people you don't want to work with. All those evils spring from the idea that something is better than nothing. The moment you go there, you compromise every standard you have.

The way most agents grow their business is to sell a piece of their soul. When you discount your commission, you give a little piece of yourself away. When you fudge a little, edit the truth in a certain way, omit something that could be relevant . . . all of these things will eat away at your personal integrity to the point of no return. It is a very slippery slope to go down.

7. REAL ESTATE IS A BATTLE FOR CONSISTENCY

What you get paid most for in this business is consistency. Not creativity, not smarts, not innovation. Those things may be important in other businesses, but as I've said, real estate isn't rocket science. It's simple. Not necessarily easy, but simple.

Consistency means going an inch wide and a mile deep—another mantra you'll see repeated in this book. Everyone wants to do the opposite, to try a little of everything to find the quick fix and get instant gratification. Forget that. Just get better at doing your job every day. This book will show you how.

And if you're worrying about technology making you obsolete, don't. That threat has always been there and always will be, so learn to live with it and leverage it. It's true, big companies are investing millions of dollars to minimize the role of the real estate agent, but they haven't done it yet. In fact, agents today are succeeding at a much higher level than they were in the past—the level of production for the top people has increased dramatically.

So far, technology hasn't changed the fact that real estate is an emotional process. As you just learned, hopes and dreams are on the line. People don't make decisions based on fact, logic, and reason. It takes a human being to help them navigate these choices. I should know—for twenty-five years, I tried to take all the emotion out of the real estate process. It doesn't work.

8. REAL ESTATE IS A THIRTY-PLUS-YEAR CAREER

Everyone comes into this business thinking about the next five minutes, the next deal. That's a recipe for disaster.

Real estate can and should be a career that lasts thirty years or more. If you do it right, you'll go through three stages. In the first decade, you'll focus on building your client base and mastering the fundamentals. In the second, you'll expand your base and optimize your processes. In the third, you'll ride the wave you've spent two decades creating.

To achieve that staying power, you need to make decisions based on the long run, not the short term. As humans, we tend to overestimate what we can do in a year and underestimate what we can do in a decade. It's unrealistic to expect quick returns. If you don't understand this, you end up in what I call the doom loop: constantly chasing leads, convincing them to hire you, and pushing them to close the deal.

That's a transactional orientation, not a relational one—and this is a relationship-based business. Building those relationships takes time, just like farming: you have to plant the seed and nurture it to get the harvest. If you don't, you'll be banging your head against the wall every day. So, stop hurting yourself. You're not getting anywhere, just running on a treadmill. The way to get off the treadmill is to build a repeat and referral business.

■ ■ ■

What I am about to say next should absolutely scare you. If you are truly committed to succeeding in this business, it should make you sit up straight and devour the rest of this book.

Imagine you are nearing the end of a three-decade career. You've sold a lot of homes over the years. In fact, most would say you've been a top performer. And yet, here you are after all this time, still chasing deals and giving your money away to get them. You're still living on the edge, always worried about whether you'll do enough business this year. You're still perpetually on call and chronically overwhelmed.

This is exactly what will happen if you don't apply the skills and put up the guardrails you'll learn in the following chapters.

No one tells you any of this on day one, and most agents never learn it. They just suffer through a few years of grueling struggle and either drop out of the rat race or resign themselves to it over the long run.

What I'm here to tell you is that doing well and being well are not mutually exclusive in real estate. In fact, unless you're doing both, you're not really succeeding. But you can't do both until you understand the reality of the business you're in and start making decisions accordingly.

Those decisions compound over time. When you make bad ones early on, they stack up against you. Let's say you discount your fee to win over a tough lead. You do it because you think in the moment that something is better than nothing, and it's just one time . . . but it's not one time. You're setting a precedent. If they refer you business or return to work with you again, you have to deal with the fact that you discounted your fee before. A discounted fee can become the gift that keeps giving, and not in a good way.

If you make great decisions instead, they stack up in your favor. Focus on the fundamentals from day one, and you'll not only save yourself a huge amount of grief but also build a strong foundation for sustained growth. Each nurtured client relationship will bring referrals, and the more of these relationships you cultivate, the faster they will snowball into a steady stream of business.

It's this power of compounding that brings wealth or poverty, not one deal. So, the sooner you start making the right decisions—based on the reality of the real estate business, not the fantasy—the sooner you'll see your business and your life transform.

2: LET GO OF FEAR

"If you want unshakable confidence, you must learn what it is like to find more fear and make a rock solid commitment not to avoid it."

—Patrick Sweeney

Real estate agents live in fear.

The fear of not knowing what to do. *What if I can't do it? What if it doesn't work? What if it takes too long?*

The fear of knocking on a door, picking up the phone, reaching out to people. *What if they think I'm pushy?*

The fear of rejection . . . the fear of discomfort . . . the fear of disappointment . . . the fear of missing out . . . the fear of failure . . .

The fear of looking foolish . . . the fear of what other people think . . . the fear of not being good enough . . . the fear of losing business . . .

The list of things to be afraid of goes on and on and on. The opportunity to be fearful is everywhere.

All that fear is unnecessary.

No one tells you this. Most people simply accept constant fear as the price they have to pay. They don't believe it's even possible to do business without it . . . but it is. There's a way of doing business that involves struggle and suffering, and a way that doesn't.

You're already familiar with the former. It includes a lot of false promises and illusions that you can get instant results, if only you find the magic formula. Unfortunately, none of that works. As you're already learning, this is a trust-based business, and you can't buy trust—you have to earn it.

But you *can* do that with no fear or stress. That's not a false promise.

The problem with fear isn't that it exists. It's that you run from it, avoid it, look away from it. In that way, you're letting it run your life. We get so used to living in fear that we don't even realize how much it's impacting us every day. Fear keeps you locked in a fight for survival, and when you're fighting to survive, you can't thrive.

This chapter isn't about overcoming fear. This is not a battle— you're not trying to kill fear. You just need to examine it and let it go. In that way, fear can be turned to your advantage.

FEAR IS A FEELING

We are hardwired to see the world as a dangerous place. It's in our DNA. It's the survival instinct—fight, flee, or freeze. Fear is what the most primitive part of our brains wants us to pay attention to because that's how we stay alive.

But what is fear, actually?

Simply put, fear is a feeling. It is not a fact. It's you deciding there is the threat of danger in the future, near or distant. The moment you travel just outside your comfort zone, fear shows up, causing you to experience some level of discomfort physically, emotionally, mentally, spiritually, or all of the above. The feeling may be mild or very intense depending on what you perceive is "at risk" at that moment.

This danger is a story you tell yourself, although it feels very real in the moment. When some event or circumstance triggers a painful memory of the past or uncertainty about the future, you immediately anticipate some form of suffering and want to protect yourself. These stories can be incredibly convincing—so convincing that most of the time, you don't even question them.

That's because your survival-based mind *wants* you to be afraid. It doesn't care about happiness, fulfillment, love, or joy. It only cares whether you are passing your genes to the next generation or not. There is a good chance your survival-based mind is holding you prisoner right now.

But here's the crazy part: this imprisonment is self-imposed. Fear is something you do to yourself. No person, no situation can *make* you afraid. Fear is something you *choose* to experience. After all, you are the one telling yourself those stories in your head . . . and you can choose not to.

FEAR IS RUNNING YOUR LIFE

If you don't know fear is running your life, *fear is running your life*.

Everything agents do in life and business is to compensate for their fears. Just look at the chase—convince—close doom loop I talked about in the last chapter, which virtually every agent gets stuck in. Why chase leads? You're afraid of missing out. Why convince them? You're afraid they won't make the "right" choice. Why push them to close the deal? You're afraid they won't do what you want them to do.

And the biggest fear of all? If you put yourself out there without any defenses, you'll get rejected.

This goes back to the basic instinct for acceptance and belonging. Humans depend on each other for survival; ten thousand years ago, rejection by the tribe meant death. So, your survival brain tells you that being open and vulnerable puts you in danger.

In reality, it makes you strong. You're most attractive to others when you're honest and authentic, not when you're putting up a front to protect your feelings. Putting yourself out there is the absolute best way to make genuine connections with others, which, as you learned in Chapter 1, is a crucial step in turning contacts into sales.

This is just one example of how fear limits your ability to take action. It makes you drive through life with the brakes on, always waiting for something bad to happen. And when you're living with the brakes on, it's impossible to ever find out what you're truly capable of.

The fact is, worrying about the future never changes anything for the better. Either it turns out to be not as bad as you thought, so you suffered unnecessarily by anticipating a bad outcome . . . or it turns out bad, and you doubled your suffering by worrying about it in advance.

People often resist this idea. They think, *If I'm worry-free, I'll get lazy—I won't have the motivation or urgency to do the things I need to do.* It's true, fear can be a motivator sometimes, like when the threat of a rabid bear motivates you to run for your life. In practice, though, fear is far more likely to paralyze than energize you.

You know what else can motivate you? Serving the moment in front of you. Elevating it and enjoying it. If we fully embrace the idea that life is a miracle and we are here to experience as much life as possible, not pick and choose what we want and don't want, this approach will completely change what it feels like to be a human being on this planet.

This is why dealing with your fears is so important. As an adult, you can reinforce your childhood survival responses of fight, flee, or freeze . . . or you can begin to reprogram your mind.

FEAR CAN BE YOUR FRIEND

In his bestselling book *Take the Stairs*, Rory Vaden tells a story about buffalo and cows in the Rocky Mountains. The two animals may seem similar in many ways, but when a storm blows in, they don't behave similarly at all. The cow tries to avoid the storm by running away from it. However, this only prolongs the time it spends under the storm, exposed to the rain, wind, and snow. In contrast, the buffalo runs *into* the storm. By facing the winds head-on, the buffalo passes through the storm faster and ultimately suffers less than the cow.

This story has been shared repeatedly, and whether it's true or not, it illustrates a crucial choice we all face constantly. Are you going to run from your fears or face them?

Most people run. They avoid doing or even thinking about the things they're afraid of, and they'll go to great lengths to do so. People who are afraid of flying will drive for days to avoid it, and even miss out on important family events and life-changing opportunities. I talk to agents every day who are so afraid of reaching out to people they know that they'd rather spend ten times more effort trying to turn strangers—like low-quality internet leads—into clients.

The basic logic behind running from your fears is that if you avoid them, you'll minimize your pain and suffering. THIS IS A LIE. Just because you imagine something might cause discomfort doesn't mean it actually will—and just because it causes discomfort doesn't mean it won't also lead to the outcomes you want.

In reality, most of the things we worry about never even happen, and if they do happen, the pain they cause is far less than we imagine. Let's say you're afraid to call a past client you've neglected for years because you think they'll criticize you or get angry. I can tell you from experience that most of them won't—they'll be perfectly gracious, maybe even genuinely happy to hear from you.

One of the coaching exercises I ask clients to do is reach out to past clients they haven't spoken to in a long time. Most resist at first. When they finally do reach out (because I keep my thumb in their back until they do), the response is overwhelming: "I can't believe you called, it is so great to hear from you."

Agents are leaving thousands and thousands of dollars on the table by not staying connected to their past clients and sphere, and the only reason why is FEAR. This is another example of how fear runs your life and you don't even know it. This is a big deal, and more importantly, it is an unforced error (more on this in Chapter 6).

And what if you call and they do reject you? What if they say you're the worst agent ever and hang up on you? You might feel a bit down for a few minutes, but really, what does it matter? You know the cliché: what doesn't kill you makes you stronger. You didn't lose a friend. You didn't even lose a client—you had already lost them long before you made the call. That person couldn't have meant much to you if you failed to make contact for years, so you haven't really lost anything at all, except the fantasy of a possible deal in the future. You'll get over it quickly.

So, as you can see, fear is not a reliable indicator of future pain. In fact, most of the time, it's an indicator of *opportunity*. That's the uncanny thing about fear: it almost always points you exactly in the direction you need to go.

The math here is very simple. To succeed in life, you must risk failure; success and failure are two sides of the same coin. In fact, you will only succeed up to the point you are willing to risk failure.

If you do not have the guts to fail, you will never know what it means to play at your highest level. Your fear points to the risks you must take to achieve what you have never achieved before.

When you understand fear this way, it becomes something that gives you focus and energy instead of smothering your gut instincts and intuition. There's no reason to avoid it—you need *more* of it in your life, not less, because it's propelling you in the right direction.

Now, I'm not saying you need to rush headlong into your fear like a charging buffalo. Instead, the idea is to embrace it, address it, and let it go. This means intentionally going outside your comfort zone and learning to flip your fear into positive action on a consistent basis. The more you do this, the more opportunities you open for yourself, and the richer your life will be.

I know that as a real estate professional, you want to sell more homes. I also know you're forever searching for an easier, simpler, and faster way of getting results. The answer to this pursuit is *not* going to be found in magic pills, shortcuts, or gimmicks. Those are just ways to avoid your fears.

You can make a different choice: put all your fears out on the table and see what's really there. What are you so afraid of? And what if, instead of running from those fears, you tried moving toward them with courage, curiosity, and confidence?

For example, one of my coaching clients had two regrets eating at him for a long time. In one situation, he had gotten a referral for a listing from one of his past clients. He sold the new client's home, but in the end, there was a problem with the deal that was never really resolved. He felt so bad about it that he was afraid to stay in touch with the person who had made the referral . . . and six years later, he was still thinking about it.

On top of that, he and his assistant had clashed over a major disagreement, and he had fired her in front of everyone. He didn't regret the decision to part ways, but he did regret the disrespectful way he had done it. Now she lived in the same neighborhood, and he was afraid of running into her, to the point where he avoided the local grocery store and Starbucks.

I told him to call both of them. It took a few weeks, but he finally did it. The former client didn't pick up, so he left a message asking for a callback. The former assistant didn't pick up either, but he apologized in the voicemail. She called him back, and they cleared the air. He felt a thousand pounds lighter. He had been carrying that fear around for so long, and when he finally examined and addressed it, it was like setting himself free.

Sometimes it turns out the way you want, and sometimes it doesn't. Either way, it's okay. What's not okay is holding onto the fear.

EXAMINE YOUR FEARS . . . AND LET THEM GO

I am not saying all this as some kind of paragon of fearlessness. I lived more than sixty years in fear before I understood what I'm telling you now. It sucked. It wasn't fun.

I didn't want to struggle or suffer anymore, so I learned to rewire my brain's response to fear. You can do this faster than you think; once you develop an awareness of fear, your behavior changes quickly.

Step 1: Recognize the Presence of Fear

Don't judge it, or yourself. Just recognize that it's there. Fear is a feeling, and you're experiencing that feeling. Don't try to suppress it—fear only has power when it's kept in the dark.

So, bring it out into the light. Examine it and ask: What exactly do you fear will happen?

Then, run your fear through the filter of opportunity. What will happen if you move in the direction of your fear? What are you not seeing or considering because of your fear? What opportunity is disguised here as something to fear?

Step 2: Make a Commitment That There's Nothing to Fear

Nothing in life is to be feared . . . only to be understood.

This probably sounds crazy. What do I mean by nothing is to be feared? Shouldn't we fear pain and suffering? Shouldn't we fear death?

Well, look at your own life. Have you experienced any pain or suffering? Of course you have—we all have. And yet, you're still here. You made it through, and you might even be a better and stronger person for it. There is little, if anything, that you can't handle. So, nothing to fear there.

And as for death, it is simply a fact of life. Death will happen to all of us, and it is random and unpredictable. When it happens to you, you won't be around afterward to experience the consequences. After you leave, a few people will probably feel some pain for a while, but as we've just established, pain is nothing to fear. And as for the rest of the universe, it will go on without you, just as it did before you.

You can choose to cling to the fear of pain and death—and most people do—but there is no *should* or *must* about it. Pain and death are inevitable, and fearing them does not make them go away; it only limits your ability to achieve the success, joy, and peace you dream of.

So, why not let those fears go? Commit to the idea that there really, truly is nothing to fear—that you will be okay no matter what.

Step 3: Choose Not to Worry about What Hasn't Happened, and Deal with What Is Happening, Knowing You'll Be Okay

When you stop worrying about what hasn't happened yet, you free up a huge amount of mental energy to deal with what *is* happening.

And when you know that you'll be okay no matter what—because there's nothing to fear—you can deal with what's happening from a place of calm instead of panic.

For me, the key to this shift was understanding that everything is temporary. No situation or emotion, good or bad, lasts forever. Life always moves on, usually faster than you expect. For example, let's say a seller is upset with you, or a deal fell apart at the last minute, or a prospect chose your top competitor over you. Something has happened, and you feel uncomfortable, frustrated, disappointed, or angry.

Just let it in and let it go. Failure isn't fatal, and success isn't forever. No one deal will change your life. And remember, you've been through pain and suffering before, and you're still here—that's how you know you'll be okay.

You don't need to fear a tough conversation; just have it and let it go. Instead of resisting or avoiding the unpleasantness, you can simply allow it to happen. It will be over quickly.

You don't even need to fear losing a client. It happens; it's okay. There will be others. Remember in the beginning, when you had *no* clients? You made it here from there, and you could do it again if you had to.

In this whole process of responding to your fears, what you're really doing is letting go of the need for control. Most people operate under the illusion that maintaining control is how you get the best outcome in whatever you're trying to do. In truth, trying to control everything is a waste of energy that only blocks things from getting done.

I learned this in the process of creating my first book, in collaboration with my coauthor, Chris Voss, and a ghostwriter. At first, I did a lot of hands-on editing and was deeply concerned with getting everything just right. After months of struggle, I finally realized I was getting in my own way. I recognized that the book didn't have to be perfect; in fact, perfection was impossible, and my pursuit of it would only prevent the book from ever getting written. Once I let go of the need for control, I experienced a lot less friction, and the book got done quickly.

The same is true of my coaching business. When I first started and built up a staff, I micromanaged everyone. I needed things done in a certain way. It took me a long time to realize how immature and limiting this style of management is. When you loosen your death grip on the wheel and stop trying to have your way at every turn, business and life become a lot easier and more enjoyable.

Bottom line: your fears show you the direction you need to go. Embracing them expands your life; resisting them shrinks it. You need more fear in your life, not less.

The ability to embrace your fears is a muscle you must build over time. It starts with awareness, and it grows with practice. Lean in, not away. Welcome what is unknown and uncertain. Be curious. Be courageous. Be confident.

You might think it can't be that simple . . . but it is.

■ ■ ■

When I coach people on this, I get a *ton* of resistance. Everyone wants to know what else they can do instead . . . but there is no other option. The only thing you need to do is let go of your fear. If you don't, nothing else is going to change. Fear will continue running your life, for the rest of your life.

That would be a real shame, because there is something unique and special about you: No one has ever walked your exact path in life. No one will ever walk the same steps that await you. You are indeed one of a kind. There is no other person on planet earth like you. You are genuinely an "energy" like no other.

And this "energy" is your life force—the same life force that created the universe and everything that has ever been and will ever be. This life force is waiting to flow up and through you and touch the world in every way possible. It's waiting to infuse love and joy and bliss into your every moment.

Before you dismiss that idea as corny or crazy, consider this: What's stopping that flow is nothing more than fear . . . and fear has been running your life for as long as you can remember. Is it impossible to imagine that life might be radically different if you take a radically different approach to fear?

Fear and worry don't leave room for happiness or joy. So, with each fear you confront, you unlock more and more positive energy. I know this seems hard, but it's really not. It can happen in an instant. Your fears can only live in a space of inaction, and when you deconstruct them properly, they lead you to the right actions. The action replaces the fear.

Isn't that ironic? We don't fear what's bad for us—we fear what's good for us. Those fears are actually a call to action, and in taking action, we eliminate the fear.

So, get ready to take on the next fear. Challenge every single fear you have. In fact, challenge every belief you have about you, the universe, and others.

Only you are standing in your own way. No one is doing it to you, and no one is going to do it for you. On this side of your fears, you'll find survival and nothing more. On the other side of your fears, you'll find *life*.

3: BE COACHABLE

One of my best coaching clients, Elaine Stucy, came to me before she even got started in real estate. She was in network marketing, and she had heard about me from a friend and figured I might be able to help her grow her business. From our conversation, I could tell that she had the potential to make a lot of money in real estate, and I strongly encouraged her to make a career change. "Funny you should say that," she replied, "because I actually do have a real estate license."

She took my advice, and within two weeks, she had set up her new business. She did everything I said: She knocked on doors, focused on being a listing agent, studied her scripts and dialogues, charged a full fee, and hired an assistant. She took my coaching . . . all of it. She didn't resist or push back in any way. She had a huge desire to succeed and simply did what I asked her to do. As a result, she built an incredible business and a seven-figure income.

Another outstanding client, Stephanie, also started with me from ground zero of her business. I met her when she had just joined Coldwell Banker, and I was teaching a course to new agents called Fast Start. She had no experience or network, but she did have a fierce eagerness to learn and challenge herself on a daily basis.

Like Elaine, she did everything I said . . . and today, she has thirty people on her team and closes over 250 transactions per year.

I say these people are two of my best clients not because they're the most successful on paper but because they're the most *coachable*. They do what I teach them. They always seek to improve. And they embrace the inevitable discomfort that comes along with that.

I cannot help you—this book cannot help you—if you don't want to be coachable. First and foremost, that means *doing what you're told.*

I cannot stress this enough. I know you got into the business because you wanted to be your own boss and not have to report to someone. Please understand that is a surefire recipe for failure for most agents. Do what your coach asks you to do. That's what a player–coach relationship is. You're wasting your time and money if you don't do what your coach says.

That doesn't mean you *have* to do what I'm teaching in this book. You don't *have* to do anything in life. But if you want to build a thriving real estate business with no stress and great quality of life, this is the only way I know of—and as I said earlier, I've coached more agents one-on-one than anybody on Earth. In 60,000 hours of coaching, there's not much I haven't seen.

This is the part everyone wants to skip over. Don't.

I know what you're thinking: *Just give me the information—I don't need a bunch of mindset crap.* But let's be very clear on one thing: everything starts with mindset. If you don't get your head on straight, nothing else matters. This is not something you can gloss over. This is where the coaching starts. It's your first test of being coachable. If you're thinking you can just fast forward past this chapter, it's a strong indication you may not be as coachable as you think you are.

If you think you already know what's best for you, you don't need me. If you've already decided what's going to work and what's not, I have no value. If you're not going to do what I ask, I can't help you.

I'm writing for people who want to get better. To do that, you have to start by being open, willing, and ready to learn. So, I'm asking you to trust your coach and be 100 percent committed to what you're receiving. If you're not, you may as well put this book down right now. If you are, this chapter will teach you how to be coachable.

DO WHAT YOU'RE TOLD

I joke all the time: just once, I'd love for someone to do what I ask them to do.

As an athlete, starting at a very early age, I was coached. I always did exactly what I was told to do. I never questioned my coaches. I took their word as the gospel. Go to any sports team and see: The coach's words are not suggestions. They're not ideas. They're commands, and good players follow them without resistance. Your coach tells you what to do, and you do it—it's that simple.

Most real estate agents are missing this skill. They don't get that coaching isn't an a la carte menu where they get to pick what they like. They insist on doing what they want to do—what feels comfortable—and avoiding what's uncomfortable.

Sadly, they're shooting themselves in the foot. There's a *reason* the coach calls the shots. In sports, good coaches have seen far more of the game and thought far more about how to win than any single player. They have the clearest view of not just the big picture but also each individual player's strengths, weaknesses, and potential. This puts them in a much better position than the players to craft a winning strategy.

It's the same in real estate. You, as an individual, have an extremely limited view. You barely get a glimpse of your own market, let alone the industry as a whole. You don't know what other people are doing or how well it's working for them. If you're like most agents, you don't even know how well your own choices are working for you. You're too busy doing the work to analyze it all.

That's what your coach is for: to analyze you, along with all the other players, and figure out the strategy and tactics that will give you the best chance of success. My job is very clear and straightforward: **to position you to live and work at your highest and best**. Period, end of story. I can't do the work for you.

None of this is about your feelings.

You want to sell houses, right? (I hope you truly want that, or you're reading the wrong book.) To sell houses, you have to do things that aren't necessarily enjoyable. I know you just want to put someone under contract quickly. Nobody wants to work on their mindset, time block, do what their CRM tells them to do, build process into every part of their business, master their sales skills, or know their numbers . . . but that's what it takes to build a lasting business. If you were hoping for a different option, I'm very sorry to burst your bubble.

And in any case, all the reasons why you don't want to do something are just stories you're telling yourself. As you learned in Chapter 2, you can *let go* of those stories. You're the one telling them, and you can choose to stop.

Most people are waiting to hear something they *want* to do. My favorite question (and I get this all the time) is, "What else can I do?" It's code for, "I'm not gonna do anything you've asked me to do so far. Give me another option." Everyone wants to pick and choose the pieces they like about the strategy and throw away the rest.

It doesn't work that way. What I'm giving you in this book is a package deal; if you want it to work, you have to do all of it. It's not a collection of advice; it's a system, and systems only work when all the parts are present. So, there is no "what else." This is it. If you pick the system apart, you destroy its integrity.

Not long ago, one of my coaching clients told me about another client who was doing exactly that—picking the system apart. He had been working with me for about a year, and he said he liked a lot of what I was saying, but he didn't necessarily agree with it all. In particular, he resisted the concept of the Favorite or the Fool and the idea that you shouldn't waste time on listing appointments you have no chance of winning. "I think that can work for an experienced agent," he said, "but I don't care if I only have a 20 percent chance. I want to go on the appointment."

This is the nonsense that stops people from realizing their potential. I don't need you to like or agree with everything I tell you to do. I just need you to do it—ALL of it. I know this probably sounds very harsh. That's coaching. This is not a debate.

You don't need to come up with ideas. I've put a lot more hours into thinking about what you need to do than you have. I never, ever went up to any of my coaches and said, "Hey coach, I think I have a better idea." Maybe Tom Brady did that (or not), but he earned that right—he didn't start out that way.

So, pay attention. Eyes wide open. I'm not just saying stuff. I'm not here to torture you or make your life hard—I'm here to make your life better. Everything I say in this book has been thought about deeply and extensively, and it made the cut because you need it. So, just do it.

GET BETTER EVERY DAY

Doing what you're told is step one, but being coachable also means working to improve every day. Otherwise, doing what you're told becomes like doing chores—like a teenager dragging their feet and rolling their eyes while taking out the trash.

That's not what we're going for here. You need to be like the athlete who puts maximum effort into every workout, or the musician who makes the most out of every minute of practice—fully committed. You don't have to make massive progress with each step. Just aim to get a little better every single day. That's how you get a lot better over a long time.

I like to think of it in terms of a concept from Japanese martial arts called Shu-Ha-Ri. These are the three stages of learning and growth.

In the first stage, Shu, I don't want you to think. Do what you're told without thinking. You can ask questions about how to do it, but don't question why. In the next stage, Ha, you can start thinking about what you're doing and asking deeper questions. Understand why you're doing it so you can get better at it. Only in the final stage, Ri, do you begin to put your personal spin on it. This is only possible once you have mastered the skill in its original form.

This is exactly what I went through when I first learned about Tactical Empathy from Chris Voss. His first book, *Never Split the Difference*, is about using Tactical Empathy to be a more effective negotiator, and I immediately saw the potential to apply it in real estate. When Chris and I first started working together, I had to simply do what I was told—which included saying and doing a lot of things that seemed unnatural at first. It was uncomfortable, even scary at times.

Over time, I became more comfortable and started thinking more deeply about what I was doing. I watched my coaching clients apply these new ideas and analyzed the results. I began to understand not just what to do, but how and why it worked. Only after several years of constant, dedicated practice did I start to come to Chris with my own creative twists on his ideas, tweaking and adjusting them for the real estate context. That's when we wrote our book, *The Full Fee Agent*, which teaches real estate agents how to use Tactical Empathy to transform their businesses.

When it comes to Shu-Ha-Ri, one of the hardest lessons for people to learn is this: until you're doing it, there is nothing to ask.

Everyone wants to ask questions before they begin. I tell them what to do, and before they make even one attempt, they have questions. *What if . . . ? What about . . . ? How do I . . . ?* They get in their own heads, imagining objections and complications that haven't happened yet and probably will never happen. They get stuck in stories that aren't real. Creating obstacles that don't exist is a bad habit to develop.

This happened when I first introduced Tactical Empathy to my coaching clients. No one had ever tried this in real estate before. We had no proof of anything—just faith in the fundamental logic of the theory and evidence of its power in other contexts. Everyone had a million questions and doubts; only a few people were willing to just do it, no questions asked. Without them, we never would have gotten anywhere.

It reminds me of this quote from Theodore Roosevelt:

It is not the critic who counts; not the man who points out how the strong man stumbles, or where the doer of deeds could have done them better. The credit belongs to the man who is actually in the arena, whose face is marred by dust and sweat and blood; who strives valiantly; who errs, who comes short again and again, because there is no effort without error and shortcoming; but who does actually strive to do the deeds; who knows great enthusiasms, the great devotions; who spends himself in a worthy cause; who at the best knows in the end the triumph of high achievement, and who at the worst, if he fails, at least fails while daring greatly, so that his place shall never be with those cold and timid souls who neither know victory nor defeat.

You can only learn real estate by doing. You can't learn from the sidelines. Don't expect miracles the first time you try something new—you have to be willing to fall down, and you will fall, repeatedly. Just get back up and go again.

PUT IN THE REPS

At the core of Shu-Ha-Ri is the idea of deliberate practice. I'm asking you to rewire the way you do business, to rewire your brain . . . in essence, to build six new habits, one for each of the six building blocks.

I say "habits" because we really are creatures of habit. Ninety-five percent of what we do every day, we do on autopilot. Only 5 percent is decided by the fully conscious mind.

Autopilot is driven by your programming, which is determined very early in life, from birth to about age seven. At that age, our brains can't yet make judgments about whether the information coming in is good or true or worth keeping. So whatever our parents, teachers, and peers show us, intentionally or otherwise, we learn. Sadly, most of us end up programmed to believe that we're not good enough and that the world is a dangerous place.

Your habit mind is the voice going off in your head 24/7, and it's much more powerful than your conscious mind. In fact, when people overthink, they're not really thinking at all. They're just listening to their programming. Your conscious mind might be telling you one thing, but your habit mind's programming doesn't support that, so guess which one wins?

That's why it's so hard to change your behavior. Your conscious mind is flexible; it's where you think, imagine, create, and set goals. It can learn from everything—a book, seminar, conversation, observations. But your habit mind is different. It's like a software program that just runs over and over. The only way to change it is to uninstall the old habits and install new ones.

Most of the time, people focus on solving problems at the conscious level and never realize how their habits are undermining their efforts. This happens *a lot* with money, for example. Lots of people are programmed from childhood to believe that money is scarce and hard to get. They spend most of their lives worrying about it or trying to make more of it. What they don't do is work to change the root cause of the problem—the programming. So, even if they make more money, at some point they'll be right back to worrying about money again.

Until you have habits that support what your conscious mind wants, your goals will remain out of reach. This is where the six building blocks come in. They are six new programs for your habit mind.

So, how do you install a new habit? You just *do it*.

This may sound simplistic or dismissive. After all, there are whole books about building habits. But no amount of reading or thinking will get you anywhere. That's not how the habit mind learns. The only way to replace a habit is to *do* the new behavior over and over, and *stop* doing the old one.

It starts with awareness. You have to be aware of the behavior you want to change, when it happens, and what enables it to happen. Many times, you can adjust your environment to make it harder to engage in the old behavior and easier to practice the new one. You can create nudges to remind yourself what to do and guardrails to keep you on track.

But in the end, the only way to install a new habit is through repetition.

The Four Stages of Competence model, introduced by Noel Burch in the 1970s, sums up this process of habit building very succinctly:

- Stage 1: Unconscious Incompetence
- Stage 2: Conscious Incompetence

- Stage 3: Conscious Competence
- Stage 4: Unconscious Competence

You must pass through each stage intentionally and methodically. Progress only happens over time.

Every time you perform a behavior correctly, you strengthen the neural pathways that define that behavior in your brain. The stronger those pathways become, the more automatic the behavior gets, until it ceases to be awkward and becomes your default. That's what allows you to do that behavior effectively even when you're under pressure, as real estate agents so often are.

Notice I said every time you perform a behavior *correctly*. Doing it poorly doesn't help—it just reinforces the wrong neural pathway. That's why the standard of perfection is so important. You'll never achieve perfection, but you must always aim for it. Aim to get it right, every time. When you make a mistake, stop and correct it. Don't let yourself keep repeating the same errors, or you'll end up getting great at the wrong thing.

Vince Lombardi, one of the greatest coaches in the history of sports, said it best: "We will chase perfection, and we will chase it relentlessly, knowing all the while we can never attain it. But along the way, we shall catch excellence."

To make new neural pathways, you don't just have to practice the new skills. You also have to *stop* practicing the old skills. They cannot coexist, or the old ways will always outcompete the new ways simply because they've been programmed into your brain for longer. To truly change the way you do business, you *must* give up your old habits.

This will be hard, especially if you feel you've already achieved some measure of success. You won't want to risk losing what you've already gained. But you have to abandon what works okay to make room for what works great.

Tiger Woods had the courage to do that. He won his first PGA Masters in 1997 by a huge margin, but immediately afterward, he went back to his coach and redeveloped his entire swing. It took a whole year to hit the ball *once* the way he envisioned it. Then it took another six months to lock in the new swing until it became automatic. In the meantime, the press and everyone else were doubting him and writing him off. He then went on to win seventeen PGA tournaments in 1999 and 2000. *That* is commitment!

The same will be true for you. You must recognize what doesn't work and let go of your fear and hope. Keep working at the new behavior until it truly becomes second nature. There is no other option.

Your habit mind is going to fight you hard. You will be tempted to give up many times. The old programming will play mental tricks on you. You must stay committed to the new way of doing things until the groove you are carving out is deep enough and the momentum great enough to override the old way, even on autopilot. This process is absolutely critical to your success, and it's all about doing, not thinking.

As you put in your reps, focus on the process itself, not your goals. Your goals aren't helping you learn. In fact, they're what's preventing you from achieving your goals. It's counterintuitive, but it makes perfect sense. Obsessing over results takes your mind away from the process, and the process is what leads to results. The harder you press and chase, the farther you get from the outcome you want.

It's not about getting it done; it's about doing it every day. It's not about achieving a certain level of production; it's about improving a little each time. Results are simply feedback. Are you moving in the right direction or not? Your only goal is to be smarter today than you were yesterday because you learned from what you did yesterday. You're putting in the reps.

EMBRACE DISCOMFORT

During my rookie year in training camp with the Dolphins, we did a one-on-one pass coverage drill every day. It highlighted my weakness as a player: I was strong against the run, but not so much against the pass. Every day I would get in the back of the line, hoping I would only have to go once or maybe not at all.

Then one day, I woke up and said to myself, *What am I doing? I won't get any better by getting in the back of the line.* So, I started going to the front of the line, and I got aggressive. I started playing to win instead of playing not to not lose. Over the course of the year, I was still uncomfortable, but that discomfort was no longer getting in my way. My skills were improving every week, and I was gaining more and more confidence.

It's just like the cow and buffalo you read about in Chapter 2. Instead of running away, I ran toward what made me uncomfortable. I turned my anxiousness into a different energy. Instead of being timid, I got bold. It was the classic fake-it-until-you-make-it mindset. You're going to have to do this over and over if you want to implement what I teach in this book.

Virtually every single one of my coaching clients struggles with getting uncomfortable on purpose. Every night I do a role-play call with one hundred agents. I ask who wants to go over a scenario—for example, the commission conversation, or breaking bad news to a client, or calling to reconnect with past clients.

I always get crickets. I get it—there's a lot of pressure when you're in the hot seat, even more than when you're talking to a client, because all your peers are listening. You're afraid they're going to judge you and think poorly of you.

It's uncomfortable, and yet it's 100 percent necessary because you shouldn't be "practicing" on your clients. You need to practice in a place where the stakes are low and you can get the feedback you need to improve. When you have those opportunities, make the most of them. Be prepared to give your best effort; don't just make stuff up on the fly.

Most importantly, don't get defensive; that defeats the whole purpose of the exercise. When my clients are on the hot seat, I can be very direct in my coaching. My job is **not** to coddle or babysit and give accolades for trying. This is not a cheerleading session. It is coaching. If you are thin-skinned and take things personally, you will not hear any coaching, only criticism.

In the NFL, our every move was scrutinized. Every practice was filmed, and afterward, we watched the film as a team. The coach was there with the laser pointer, asking, "What were you doing there? What were you thinking?"

Embrace the discomfort. It's just another form of fear. It's just a feeling, and as you learned in Chapter 2, feelings aren't facts.

Want to know what feelings are? *Expensive.* They come and go. They don't reflect reality. And they rob you of your best opportunities to learn and grow.

I used to be very uncomfortable with public speaking, ever since an ill-fated fourth-grade piano recital when I froze and had to walk offstage. Now, public speaking is a crucial part of my profession. In the beginning, I'd be up all night before a big event, unable to sleep from the nerves, rehearsing and practicing until I was totally exhausted. My speech in the shower before any event was much better than the actual speech.

That has changed dramatically over time. I've gotten comfortable being uncomfortable. It's simply a way of being. I still get that spark of terror right before I speak, but now I love it and live for it. It makes me feel alive and tells me I'm doing the right thing: moving toward my fear, where the opportunity lies.

■ ■ ■

Being coachable is what makes learning possible. The more you fight the coaching, the slower your learning process will be. Believe me, I see it constantly. Every day, I have clients who ask me, "Do I really have to do that? Why am I doing that? Are you sure? What about this, can I do this instead?"

Just stop. STOP!! If you think you know better, why read a book or hire a coach at all?

Just recently, I got coached on how to do the audiobook narration for my previous book, *The Full Fee Agent.* The coach was telling me to do things that make no sense to me—all kinds of strange vocal exercises that felt, frankly, silly. But I trusted that if I wanted to get better, those were the things I needed to do.

Coaching is not a debate class. It's not therapy. In any competitive profession, having a coach is part of the deal because you can't see yourself. You need someone to both affirm your strengths and help you improve. You need a voice in your ear that says, "Yes you can," because the voice in your head usually says, "No you can't." You need someone who can actually see you.

Now, there's only so much coaching I can do from a book. I can only tell you what to do in a general sense. I can't hold you accountable for actually doing it. I can't make it specific to your context. I can't give you feedback on what you're doing well and what you could improve. Those things massively increase your chance of success, and I can only do them if you join the hundreds of agents who work with me every week through my one-on-one and group coaching programs (shameless plug).

But even without a live coach, what you'll learn in this book changes everything. This book is not a repeat or rehash of anything you have heard in the world of real estate training. It is a way of thinking, talking, and being. It is a wake-up call. I encourage you to really look inside yourself and decide what you are doing in this business. Are you going to be a beauty pageant participant or something different? Are you going to be a product of the "system" like most agents, or are you willing to go down a new path, as in the Life in Five Short Chapters story from Chapter 1? This book is going to make you think about your existence on many different levels.

It's not as hard as it sounds, though. When you accept that you need to do what you're told, you implicitly accept that you *can* do what you're told. No questions, no fuss. Just action—and action is what gets results.

PART II:
THE SIX BUILDING BLOCKS

4: A MINDSET OF **HARMONY**

You may not know who Napoleon Hill is, but you've almost certainly heard some derivation of his central message: "What the mind can conceive and believe, it can achieve." In other words, you can do anything you put your mind to. Where there's a will, there's a way. And on the flip side of that coin: if you want something good to happen, you have to make it happen . . . and if good things aren't happening, it's because you're doing something wrong.

This is the basis of virtually the entire self-help industry—everything from goal setting to manifestation. You've heard this message so many times from so many people throughout your life that you've probably never questioned it. You've spent your whole life working to get what you want, thinking that was the answer to a better life.

What if this is completely false?

What if constantly working to get what you want is exactly what's keeping you stuck and miserable? What if the way to achieve happiness is not to perpetually chase what you want and avoid what you don't want?

The answer to this question is the first of the six essential building blocks. It's a crucial change in the way you understand the world that will enable you to sell homes with *no stress*. Seriously, none. It's more than that, though. It's a radically different approach to life that makes it possible to enjoy your work, regardless of the problems and demands that arise constantly.

This may seem like a lot of unnecessarily deep philosophy for a book on selling real estate, but this is the *most fundamental* of the six building blocks. Remember, your goal is not just to sell more—it's to sell more in a better way, without constant overwhelm and burnout. And I promised you that you would learn to enjoy every day, no matter what. How we spend our days is how we spend our lives. Your mindset is where all that begins.

It sounds absurd, I know. A few years ago, I would have thought so too. Just suspend your disbelief for long enough to read this chapter, and you'll see that it's not crazy—it just might be the most logical thing you've ever heard in your life.

GET IN ALIGNMENT

Everything is temporary. You learned that in Chapter 2, if you didn't already know it. And look around—it's true. Nothing, not even the stars and the planets, lasts forever. The very definition of life is change.

Fortunately, change is the seed of opportunity, in life and in real estate. What makes someone buy or sell a home? Life change—a new job, marriage, divorce, kids being born, kids moving out, more money, less money, and a thousand other shifts in personal circumstances. Spoiler alert: real estate is driven by the natural flow of life.

If you want to succeed in this business for a long time, you need to get in alignment with that flow. You don't need to create or control the change. The change will happen—it's inevitable, because everything is temporary.

When it does happen, you need to be ready. Being ready means having relationships, being a trusted advisor, being competent at your job. It means being of service to those who are dealing with change. When you're in alignment with this, you're swimming in an ocean of opportunity.

But if you're like most agents, you're not in alignment. You're chasing. You have your head down and your blinders on. You are not seeing the big picture. You're trying to manufacture opportunity *now* because you've been conditioned to think that if you want something good to happen, you have to make it happen.

You're swimming against the tide instead of with it, and it slows you down. You never get anywhere. And if you keep swimming, eventually you'll drown. It's not a question of if, only when.

Why do you do this?

Because you think it will make you okay. That's what you're trying to achieve every day: just be okay. First, you figure out what would make you okay. More money, more love, fulfilling work, etc. Then, every day you go out and try to make those things happen.

The problem is, all those things are outside of you, and you have no control over the outside world. Zero. How could you? You don't control the forces of nature that shape your environment. You don't control other people. The only thing you control is yourself—how you perceive and respond to the world.

And yet, you act as if you can make things happen outside of you . . . and you feel as if everything outside of you is happening *to you.*

That makes no sense. Look at the moment in front of you now, everything around you. You didn't create this moment. It's not about you.

I know what you're thinking: *I have free will. I made choices that put me in this moment.* Yes, but the moment itself isn't happening *to you.* It is simply happening. It has nothing to do with you, so don't take it personally. The planet existed long before you and will be here long after you are gone. Unfortunately, you are not the center of the universe.

Think about it: How could the moment in front of you possibly be personal? What about the moment in front of me? Or the moment in front of someone else? Or the other eight billion people who inhabit this world? That's a lot of moments all happening at once. Do you take those moments personally? No. So why is the moment in front of *you* personal and the trillions of other moments that are happening at the very same time not personal? How can your one moment, out of all the moments taking place right now across the universe, be personal?

It's not. Life is not happening to you. It's simply happening. It's the result of natural forces interacting since the dawn of the universe, for 13.8 billion years. Those same forces created you, me, and everything that has ever existed. And because of them, you're lucky enough to be alive, here on Earth, the only place we know of where such life exists.

The mere fact of it is nothing less than a miracle. This moment is a miracle.

And yet we, in our infinite wisdom, say, "Could I have a different moment, please? I don't like this one. For me to be okay, I need a different one."

You've been doing this your entire life, and it has never worked. Yes, there are brief moments where things line up your way by chance, but they are few and far between. Mostly, you walk around resisting what the universe has put in front of you.

How long do you want to keep doing the thing that has never gotten you what you want?

This is a serious question because that's what you're doing right now. It's what most people are doing. And when people are in that mode, striving and struggling and suffering, they ask me, "What else could I be doing?"

That's the wrong question. You need to be asking, "What's stopping me from doing what needs to be done?"

The answer is simple: your personal preferences.

YOU ARE NOT YOUR MIND

There's a moment in front of you right now. As we just established, it has nothing to do with you. However, you always enter that moment with your personal preferences. You judge every moment by whether it makes you comfortable or uncomfortable. And unfortunately, there are way too many moments in life that make you uncomfortable and too few that make you comfortable.

That's the predicament you're in. If you keep approaching life this way, most of the time, you are going to struggle and suffer.

So, here's the big question: Do you want to live the rest of your life coming from love and service? Or from desire and fear?

Our whole lives, we've all been coming from desire and fear: wanting what we want and resisting what we don't, being afraid of getting what we don't want and not getting what we do want—day in and day out. It's exhausting.

The good news is, the choice is yours. You have total control over whether you live in love and service or in desire and fear. This choice has nothing to do with the outside world—it's all inside you, so it's all up to you.

You can *enjoy* every moment that unfolds in front of you. You can *serve* every moment that unfolds in front of you. And most importantly, you can make every moment *better* by being present and engaging with it.

You just need to let go of your personal preferences.

You—the essence of you—don't have any personal preferences. Your preferences reside in your mind, and you are not your mind. You've been living your whole life as if you were your mind, as if you were the voice that's in there talking every day. All those automatic thoughts, all those emotions—you've identified those things as you.

They're not. You are the *awareness* that you have a mind. You are the consciousness listening to those thoughts and feelings, not the thoughts and feelings themselves. You and your mind are two separate things. And the way to let go of your personal preferences is to create separation between yourself—your consciousness—and your mind.

Your mind is survival based. Its goal is not joy or bliss—only survival. Being okay. Your mind is the one that experiences things as either being comfortable or uncomfortable, and you've operated from your mind your entire life. But *you* are pure consciousness and awareness, which have no personal preferences.

Creating that separation and understanding it—that is the work. That is what you want to be working on every day. That is what will change your experience of life.

But that's not what you're working on. You're working on the outside world, hoping you can get it to conform to how you want things to be so you can feel better on the inside. That's never going to work, aside from fleeting moments where things happen to line up your way.

That's why you, and probably everyone you know, are suffering and struggling. No one has ever taught you any other way. Everyone is just teaching you how to be in control of things you have no control over—to set goals, to have a vision, to chase the things you think will make you okay.

There's nothing in the outside world that can make you okay. You can never have enough of anything, ever. I guarantee you. The people who are taking home $25,000 a year want $50,000. The ones who earn $50,000 want $100,000, and the $100,000 earners want $200,000 . . . all the way up to $1 million, $10 million,

$100 million, and more. The same goes for every other goal, whether it's love or houses sold. No outside circumstance is ever enough.

Being okay is strictly an inside job. You can be okay all the time, every moment of every day, but only by doing the inner work. Not the outside work.

THE INNER RIVER

What exactly is the inner work?

Michael Singer put it best when he said your mind is like a river.[1] Rivers can be smooth and calm, or they can be rough and turbulent.

Yours is turbulent right now. In fact, if you're like most agents, you're a mess—a big mess. Your mind won't shut up. The thoughts just keep coming nonstop. Your feelings, which are mostly negative, are out of control and have taken over your body. Your heart hurts even though you wish it wouldn't. You are struggling and suffering, mostly in silence.

You compare yourself. You judge yourself. Others appear to have their act together. They must be doing something you are not. You point fingers and play the blame game to console yourself.

The sense of worry just never seems to go away. You feel like you have to be on high alert all the time. The other shoe could drop at any moment. You slap a fake smile on your face and pretend you've got this, but really, you feel lost and alone in your mess . . . and you're afraid it will be this way forever.

All your consciousness is focused on the mess. Wherever you go, there it is. You are drained and exhausted. All you want is for the mess to end. You want off of this treadmill that is seemingly

---

1   *The Michael Singer Podcast*

leading you nowhere. You want a way out, but no matter what you do, it feels like too little, too late.

This is why you resort to magical thinking: What the mind can conceive and believe, it can achieve! You visualize what you want. You set your intentions. You do your affirmations. You convince yourself you can get the universe to bend to your desires. You can get more of what you want. You can avoid what you don't want. You will be happy and okay.

And then reality sinks in—really sinks in. Your powers to manifest always seem to fall short. You must be doing something wrong, or there must be something wrong with you. The clock is still ticking, getting louder and louder . . . and now you feel more lost than ever.

And this is exactly where you need to be! You are in the perfect place . . . you just don't know it.

What makes a river turbulent? Obstacles—rocks and other junk interrupting the flow of the water. The same is true of your mind. It's full of rocks, and if you can just get rid of them, you can finally have some inner peace.

Those rocks are all your favorite things: comfort, preferences, goals, magical thinking, instant gratification, hope, even fear. These are what you cling to every day. You just can't see it because you're stuck inside the rapids, holding onto the rocks. From that perspective, it seems like the rapids are coming from the outside world, constantly bombarding you with problems, and the rocks are the only things keeping you from drowning. Isn't it ironic that the things that cause you the most pain are the things you hold onto with a death grip? Life is funny that way.

That's why the first step is separation. Make space between your true self—which is pure awareness—and your mind. Get out of the water so you can sit on the bank of the river and find out what's really going on there.

When you do, you'll see that the rocks aren't saving you. They're what's causing the rapids in the first place, and you're the one who put them there. The problem is never the market or the client or any of the things you're always worrying about. It's you. It's not that there's something wrong with you or you're doing something wrong—you're just holding onto desires that conflict with reality, and reality is always going to win.

The good news is, getting rid of the rocks is easier than you think. You don't need to lift these heavy boulders out of the water. You just need to *stop holding them there*. Let them go, and the current will wash them away for you. Then the river can be restored to its natural state of calm.

There are no problems *out there*. The problem is inside you. Instead of focusing on the problem itself—the rapids (i.e., your out-of-control thoughts and emotions)—turn your attention to the source of the problem: the rocks (i.e., everything you're clinging to).

Once you've created the separation that allows you to see the rocks for what they are, you can start practicing nonresistance. You see that you're a mess—don't resist that. Don't judge yourself and beat yourself up for it. Just accept it. It's not a bad thing. In fact, it's perfect. If you weren't a mess, you wouldn't have this beautiful opportunity to grow.

Look at each rock closely. Understand what it is, and choose to stop resisting the current and just let it go. The current wants to wash it away. That's the river's natural flow. *Stop resisting*.

That's the inner work. It takes patience and diligence because you've been conditioned to resist. You've been holding on for your entire life, fighting the current and stacking up the rocks higher and higher. It will take practice to stop clinging and let it all go. You may feel totally clear one day only to come back the next and find that some rocks have returned.

That's okay. Just keep letting go.

THREE THINGS TO REMEMBER

Once again, I say all this to you not as some kind of higher being who has always lived in perfect alignment with the flow of life. Until a few years ago, I was just like you, constantly wrapped up in my desires and fears, battling against the universe with every step. Sometimes I still am.

But I learned better. Even though it sounded impossible, I opened my mind to the idea that there might be a way to enjoy every day of my life instead of struggling through them. I gave it a try, not just because it made sense to me, but because what I had been doing *wasn't working*.

Yes, I was successful on paper. I had a beautiful family, a lovely home, and a thriving business . . . but I was suffering on the inside, just like you. Just like everyone. And after sixty years of that, I was ready for something different.

Let me be clear: this is *not* optional. In the system I'm teaching you in this book, a Mindset of Harmony is not a nice-to-have. It's one of the six building blocks for a reason; without it, you can't hope to execute the other five with any kind of consistency. They'll make you uncomfortable in all kinds of ways, and if you continue letting your preferences dictate your life, you simply won't do them.

Instead, you'll be focused on fear. You'll be craving instant gratification. You will be living in a state of false hope to keep yourself going. You won't have the patience to rewire your entire way of working. You'll go straight back to doing things the way you've always done and getting the same results you always get. And then what's the point of reading any of this?

That's why it's so crucial to constantly, every moment of every day, practice nonresistance. That is what puts you in alignment with the flow of life.

The mantra of nonresistance is this: Whatever is happening is happening. None of it is personal. All of it is temporary.

Let's break that down:

1. **Whatever is happening is happening.** What you think or how you feel about it won't change the fact that it's happening. Ignoring, denying, or complaining won't make it any different. It's not inherently good or bad—it just is. You get to decide how you experience it.

2. **None of it is personal.** It only feels that way. But life is not happening to you. It's just happening. You are not a victim.

3. **All of it is temporary.** Nothing is forever. Whatever is happening now—good or bad—will pass. As Michael Singer puts it, we have willpower. We can cling to what we want . . . but it's temporary. We can resist what we don't want . . . but it's temporary. The only option left—and the best use of our free will—is to accept what is.

If you lean into those three core beliefs, life takes on a very different feel: lighter, freer, easier. It's like taking off the thousand-pound backpack you've been wearing your whole life, or taking your foot off the brake and just moving forward, without resistance.

You begin to truly understand that as a real estate agent, your job is not to make deals happen. It's to *be ready* to serve. That's what the six building blocks do: they keep you ready all the time, because you never know when the flow of life will make all the other elements align.

Being ready is a proactive process. When you live in your mind, with your preferences, you're always in a reactive state; whatever shows up, you're judging whether it makes you comfortable or uncomfortable, whether you desire or fear it, whether you should cling or resist. And in real estate, any time the slimmest possibility of a deal crosses your path, you'll chase it because you think doing another deal will make you okay. It doesn't matter whether it's a high-probability or low-probability opportunity—and most of them are low.

As a real estate professional, ask yourself this: Do you want to chase after deals for the rest of your career? Is that going to be your primary motivation? Is that going to be your driving force every day in business? Really?

Or do you want to play a different game with different rules on a different playing field?

When you know that you're going to be okay every day (because being okay doesn't depend on doing a deal), you can focus on high-probability activity (i.e., the six building blocks). And you can do this with absolutely zero fear, doubt, overwhelm, pressure, or stress.

Selling more, working less, no internal tension!

Again, all of this feels counterintuitive and unnatural at first. It seems like it's taking you away from what you want instead of toward it. But once you start actually doing it, this feeling disappears quickly. You realize that the mind you've been living in, with its survival-driven thoughts and feelings, wasn't always right. In fact, it is never right. Instead, you start to rewire your brain from survival to actually *living*.

FORGET YOUR GOALS

Still, you might be worried that if you're not trying to make something happen, you're just settling for what is. What about ambition? What about striving for better? Without my fear . . . who am I?

If I've learned one thing in thirty years, it's that in order to grow, you have to let go—and I mean let go of *everything*. What's real is that we do not control what happens in life. We do not control the tides. You may insist on swimming against them because the constant effort makes you feel like you're achieving something, but the reality is that you're going nowhere and about to drown. When you refuse to get in alignment with reality, you set yourself up to fail.

Remember, there are eight billion people on this planet. Why are your intentions and goals more important than anyone else's? Why should yours have some special ability to shape the world around you? They don't.

In fact, they don't even have the power to shape *you*. Every year in December, your manager comes in and says it's time to set goals and create a plan for next year. But no matter how much effort you put into goal setting and planning, by January 31 (or certainly no later than March 31), you've disconnected from the goal and plans. That's why most agents are stuck in a range of production, up or down 10 percent based on what the market is doing, not what they're doing.

What your goals actually do is pit your will against the universe and create the illusion that happiness will be yours soon—as soon as you reach that goal.

If you think you have to achieve your goals to be happy, you'll be waiting a long time. I played for the winningest coach in NFL history, Don Shula. Every year, his goal was always to win the Super Bowl. In thirty-two years of coaching, he achieved that goal only twice. Would it have made any sense at all for him to be unhappy for thirty years just because he didn't reach his goal?

One of my clients had a goal to reach $1 million in personal income. A couple years ago, she made it. She was stressed and overwhelmed the entire time, but she reached her goal, and she enjoyed that $1 million for about a minute.

The following year, with exactly the same effort, she closed just two homes and barely made $100K. That's real estate for you:

you have no control. The market will do what it's going to do, your goals be damned. That year, the market made her live through her worst fear. And guess what? She didn't die. She thought she would, but she lived through it, and it wasn't so bad. In some ways, it was a better year than the one before because she became a better human being.

You don't need to reach your goals to be happy. You don't need *anything* to be happy. You can live in total harmony and peace, starting now, if you just *let go.* Let go of your personal preferences. Let go of your need to control everything. Let go of the idea that more—more deals, more money, more prestige—will make you okay.

The only thing that will make you okay is letting go of all this crap so you can get in alignment with the universe. You don't get to choose what happens in life. You only get to choose how you experience it and how you respond.

The goal is to become comfortable being uncomfortable, to the point where comfort is irrelevant. Life is simply life. There's no good or bad, it's just always coming at you. Choose to enjoy it.

■ ■ ■

In the end, there are only three paths you can go down in life.

You can live in fear, running away from everything that makes you uncomfortable and existing in a constant state of worry that the next uncomfortable thing is just around the corner.

You can pit your will against the universe, trying desperately to control things that you have no control over, insisting despite all evidence that what the mind can conceive and believe, it can achieve.

Or, you can choose unconditional happiness and live in a state of harmony. You can accept each moment for what it is, without resisting or clinging to it. You can be fully present, fully engaged, and ready to give your best to whatever is in front of you.

Right now, you're in one of the first two, playing a game you can never win. *Never*. You can never outrun your fear because your survival-based mind will always create more for you, and by the very act of running, you only make your life smaller. Your will can never overcome the natural forces of the universe, no more than you can ever make the waves in the ocean obey your commands.

The question is, do you want to continue playing that game? Because there is another game you can play, and you can enjoy *every single moment* of that game. You can enjoy every single moment of your business and your life, each and every day.

Do you want to get in that game? The price of admission is incredibly high: you've got to give up all the stuff that makes you miserable. To get in the game of total happiness, joy, love, and peace, you have to let go of your desires, fears, preferences, and all the other things you cling to.

That's hard. You've been holding onto those things your whole life. In a way, you're addicted to it because the illusion of control makes you feel safe. But you're not safe—you're a mess, and you know it. And if you want to get rid of the mess, there's only one way: *let go*.

Harmony or disharmony—how do you want to live the rest of your life? Which state is more enjoyable?

Unconditional happiness or conditional happiness? You can make the choice to be unconditionally happy right now, no matter what. When you make this choice and stay committed to it, everything changes forever.

All you have to do is practice nonresistance. Every time you're experiencing some form of inner turmoil, stress, or tension, the source is always the same. You are resisting life in some way. When you drop the resistance, the negativity will disappear with it.

Let go of living in disharmony . . .

Let go of placing conditions on your happiness . . .
Let go of any and all resistance . . .
Now you can live the life you are meant to live.

5: TIME BLOCKING

hy do real estate agents work seven days a week?
Because they *don't* work five!

It's not a joke—I'm completely serious. Most agents waste their five working days on low-value activities, guided by their own fear and the demands of others. They chase dead-end leads, respond to client "emergencies," and fix mistakes they never should have made in the first place.

So, they get to the end of the week, and the important stuff didn't get done. That's why agents are forever working early mornings, late nights, and weekends. They're not working efficiently during normal work hours.

This goes back to the hope versus truth discussion. Hope is a very inefficient way to run your life. Hope is a consumer of time and energy; it takes longer and makes everything harder. Truth, on the other hand, is very efficient. It keeps things simple and is an unlimited source of time and energy.

That's why most agents are afraid to put boundaries around their time—they live in hope. They think they need all their time, every minute of every day, to get the job done. How can they take a whole day off every week, let alone every evening, if they have so much to do, and a client might need them at any time?

The problem with this thinking is that work expands to fill the time you give it. You probably already know this . . . and you also probably haven't done anything about it yet.

Time is your most precious asset, in business and in life. It's the one thing you can never get more of, and you can never save up. Once it's gone, it's gone. And yet, every day you're spending your most precious asset on other people's priorities. It makes no sense.

You need to take control of your time—and time blocking is the way to do it.

Time blocking means what gets scheduled gets done. It creates dedicated space in your week for all the activities that are most important to you, work *and* personal. By prioritizing what matters most, it forces you to focus on high-probability activities— the things that will reliably build and grow your business. That's in contrast to the random and low-priority activities most agents spend their days on, which produce little or nothing in the way of meaningful results.

As a general rule, high-probability activities include anything that builds relationships. Low-probability activities are about chasing. They're transactional, based on hope, and seeking instant gratification. Ask yourself: If you consistently engage in low-probability activities, what are your longer-term chances for success? Conversely, if you consistently engage in high-probability activities, what are your longer-term chances for success? The math is pretty clear cut.

You need to read the last paragraph over and over again. Keep reading it until this concept—high-probability activity versus chasing—gets embedded into your brain.

This is a foundational shift that dramatically changes how you do business. Chasing is purely an instinctive response to a fear-driven mindset. Think hard for a second. How can any decision made out of fear do anything more than keep your head above water? Is that your mission in life—to just get by? Is that what you are willing to settle for? Why not just start the march to your grave right now?

When you time block, you are committed to following your schedule, no matter what. If something goes in your schedule, you do it. It's not a list of suggested activities. If it's important enough to put in there, you do it. If you're not really going to do it, you don't put it in there.

This way, rather than pinballing around constantly, reacting to everything and everyone else, you stick to your schedule and do what is most important. Then, there's no need to work seven days a week—you can get everything done in five.

NO MORE CHASING

Agents struggle with time blocking more than anything else I teach. The biggest challenge is that they imagine other people's demands of their time are going to line up with their time blocks. Then, when their schedule doesn't align with someone else's, they come to the conclusion that time blocking doesn't work.

This is not a flaw of time blocking. It's a flaw in the way you are approaching time blocking.

I know what you're thinking: *What if a lead calls? What if a buyer wants to see a property now? What if a client needs me?* You think you need to be flexible enough to change your plans at any time, for anyone or anything that claims to need your attention urgently.

That's your fear talking, making you chase every "opportunity" that comes across your path, no matter how real it may or may not be. As I've already said a few times, chasing is a very ineffective way to run your business. It forces you to be on call 24/7 because you never know when someone might show up to work with you. The thing is, most of those "opportunities" are actually threats—time wasters that will never turn into business.

One of my clients wages a constant war with himself over wanting to take time off and never wanting to miss an opportunity. Every week on our one-on-one coaching call, it's the same struggle over and over again. *I hate this business because I can't take time off. I don't want to take time off because I don't want to miss a deal.* He has convinced himself that he will absolutely lose business by taking time off—never mind that this has not been his actual experience. He just imagines it has to be that way. In his mind, there is no room for the idea that taking more time off might actually lead to more business.

Here's the truth: If a person isn't willing to conform to the time you have available, they're not serious about working with you. If a buyer can't wait until your next showing time, they're not that interested in your listing. If a seller can't wait until your next prelisting appointment time, you're not the Favorite.

People who aren't willing to wait are suspects, not prospects. Your time blocks are doing you a favor by screening them out. Real prospects will conform to your schedule because they genuinely want to work with you.

Even your current, active clients don't need an immediate response 24/7. There are no life-threatening emergencies in real estate. If your own client can't wait an hour for a response from you, they don't really need your response. They'll make a decision and do whatever they need to do without your input.

It's true, time blocking forces you to say no to things. That's why agents resist it.

It's also why building block #1, a Mindset of Harmony, is *crucial* for doing it successfully. If you're still clinging to your desires, fears, and hopes, you'll want to chase everything that crosses your path. You'll be unwilling to let any "opportunity" go because your wishful thinking tells you that every opportunity is real—that if you just say and do the right things, you can turn anyone into a client.

It should be clear by now that this is a fantasy. You don't control other people. You don't "convert" them into clients through your powers of persuasion. If someone isn't willing to wait a couple of hours or days to connect with you, you never had a chance with them anyway.

The beauty of this is that time blocking and chasing are mutually exclusive. If you're unwilling to give up the chasing habit, time blocking will never work for you. On the flip side, if you believe me when I say that chasing is killing you and your business, and you want to stop, the solution is right here. Commit to time blocking, and you'll never chase again.

Instead, you'll end up working less and making more . . . and isn't that the goal?

If you think you've tried time blocking and it "didn't work" for you, I challenge you to approach it with a fresh perspective. Were you really committed to your time blocks, or did you let them get interrupted and moved around? Did you stick with it for at least a year?

If not, it's time to try again—for real this time.

HOW TO START TIME BLOCKING

Open up your calendar and start with a blank week.

We'll tackle time off first. Block out at least one day of the week, if not two or more, when you will not work. Not even a little. No email, no voicemail, no texts. You'll set up an auto-reply that you're unavailable today and will be returning calls tomorrow.

Most agents instantly break down right here. *I can't take a day off—what if I get a phone call, an email, a text?*

If that's you, I have a serious question: if you feel like you can't take *one day* a week off, why be in this business? One of the reasons you got into it was to have more freedom and flexibility. If you can't have that, you may as well do something else.

There's no perfect day to take off. Pick one or two that work best for you, and stick to your choice. Don't move them around. If you do, then before you know it, they'll disappear.

Now, let's block off personal time: everything you need for your family, kids, exercise, meditation, hobbies, errands, etc. For regular activities that have a specific time—like a workout class or school pickup—put them in the calendar. For the rest, just estimate how much time you want each day and block it out.

If you don't do this, your professional life will take over *everything*. Work will seep into every open minute you have. It's because of the survival mindset: the obsessive fear of not making enough money. That fear is always present, whether there's money in the bank or not—it's simply a bad habit. So, if you don't carve out this time first, it won't exist.

Set a start time and end time to your workday, no later than 6:00 or 7:00 p.m., maximum.

You *do not work* before the start or after the end. As we've established, you don't need those early mornings and late evenings for work. You only use them now because you're not using your day efficiently, and that's about to stop. From now on, if you can't get it done during your work hours, it doesn't need to be done.

Next, block out at least one hour a day for your CRM. One hour is the bare minimum amount of time, and you may need more depending on the size and scale of your database. You'll learn more about using your CRM in the next chapter, but for now, trust me that this is your *number one* work priority. It's more important than any client meeting. It's nothing less than the foundation of your business.

You'll use this hour to complete all the tasks your CRM tells you to do as well as any CRM cleanup that may be necessary. This is the only thing you *must* block out in your workday.

How you structure the rest of your workday is up to you. I suggest blocking out time for property showings, listing appointments, and pre-appointments because if you don't, these appointments can easily disrupt your workflow. For example, you might decide that you'll only do these appointments in the afternoons, so your morning is available for other important work.

I also recommend blocking out time for the activities that contribute to your business growth but never feel urgent—in other words, the other four building blocks. That includes honing your mindset, creating and refining your processes, practicing Tactical Empathy, and reviewing your numbers. If you don't set aside specific times for these things, they will probably never happen.

Setting up your calendar with time blocks is the easy part. Now, you have to actually respect them, which is where most people break down. To be successful with this, there are three things you must do.

First, don't move the time blocks. Do what you said you would do when you said you would do it. As soon as you start shuffling time blocks around, you will perceive them as optional. They are not. That's the whole point of this practice.

Second, don't put things in your calendar that you're not going to do. Your calendar isn't just your plan—it's your commitment. If it's in there, you're doing it, and that's that. So if you don't 100 percent intend to follow through, it doesn't belong there.

Third, stop spending time thinking about things you're not going to do. That takes up a huge amount of mental space and derails your focus from the things you've committed to. Either you're doing it, and it goes in your calendar, or you're not, and it doesn't get any of your time.

If you do those three things, time blocking will radically change your life and business for the better.

EVERYONE CAN TIME BLOCK

Everyone—yes, even you—can do this.

Here's how I know: Everyone I coach shows up on time for their call. When they have listing appointments, they show up on time for those, too. Unexpected things happen in life, and yet, they always make those two things work. No matter how busy an agent is, they always have time to go on a listing appointment.

The problem is, they just don't treat their time blocks like listing appointments. They don't give their time blocks the same sense of importance and immutability.

People make excuses for this. *Steve, you don't get my life. My life is different.* No, it's not. Everyone is busy. Everyone has things come up. You're not special. There is no reason this cannot work for you.

In fact, the busier an agent gets, the more they see time blocking as a necessity because they learn to *value* their time. Top performers know that time is the one resource that's truly finite, and therefore it's the most precious one. So many people are making demands on their time that they *have* to schedule everything, or their most precious resource will be used up before the important stuff gets done.

In contrast, most agents value money over time. They're always telling me they need more money. Well, the reason they're in that situation is because they're not valuing their time. They're giving it away, wasting it on unproductive activities, hoping for short-term results instead of building a business for the long term.

It's easy to understand this intellectually, but translating it into behavior is hard. Your habit of reacting to every demand in real time is deeply ingrained. That's why time blocking is so important—it puts clear rules on your time-spending behavior. There's no wiggle room to slide back into your old ways.

I learned time blocking at an early age with sports. Practices and games take place at a certain time, and you have to be there, no excuses. In the NFL, every minute of every day is time blocked with practices, workouts, team meetings, and more.

Nowadays, my life is time blocked from 5:00 a.m. to 7:00 p.m. You may hear that and think it sounds restrictive to be so inflexible . . . but it's the opposite. It's pure freedom because I wake up every day never having to wonder what I'm going to do. I never have to spend my mental or emotional energy deciding how to spend my day. I don't wrestle with questions of what I *should* do or *feel like* doing. I just roll out of bed at 4:58 a.m. and get on the phone at 5:00 a.m. I don't have to *feel like* getting on the phone at 5:00 a.m. It's not about my feelings—it's about my schedule.

As I've said before, feelings are expensive. If you're going to let them guide your decisions, you better believe it will cost you in your business, because what you feel like doing has nothing to do with what needs to be done. Most of the time, there's not much alignment there. When your feelings are in charge, you will spend most of your time doing something other than what actually makes money for your business.

Time blocking makes that impossible by taking your feelings out of the equation entirely. You don't have to consult them at all. Just do what the calendar says, period.

I have twenty-eight half-hour time blocks each day. I view each one as a moneymaking opportunity, and my goal every day is to fill up each one with something that will make money. Just by looking at my calendar, I can see if I'm making money this week or not. And

I've learned to do all my non-moneymaking "work" in the gaps that open up when calls get canceled or end early. That's when I send an email, make an invoice, respond to someone, or brainstorm.

As an agent, you don't make money by the hour, but there is still a clear set of activities that relate directly to earning a commission: anything that fits into the progression I introduced in Chapter 1. That includes making contacts, creating connections, nurturing relationships, talking with leads, interacting with clients, and all the things that go into helping buyers and sellers find each other and make deals.

Don't make the mistake of thinking that things like cultivating your mindset and refining your processes aren't moneymaking activities. Of course they are—they are what enables you to build strong, genuine relationships and deliver excellent client experiences. They elevate the quality and effectiveness of everything else you do, so don't leave them out just because they don't involve direct contact with clients and prospects.

If you're still resisting the idea of time blocking, let me ask you this: Are you building a business or just chasing a deal?

It's a conscious choice. If you don't use time blocking, you'll chase, which is mutually exclusive with building a business. Chasing comes from a place of fear—*If I miss a deal, I might not get another chance, and then I'll go broke and die.* It's also what makes you work 24/7, which is *not* the idea you had when you decided to get into real estate.

Building a business can only happen from a place of trust—*I will do what needs to be done for my business, when it needs to be done, and not get distracted by other people's priorities; if someone is serious about doing business with me, they will wait.* Time blocking is the key to making this happen. It's the only way you can take control of your most precious asset and actually *choose* how much you want to work.

■ ■ ■

Most agents are pushing a boulder up a hill every day. They chase deals in search of short-term success, allowing everyone and everything to make claims on their time and energy, and their only solution is to just keep pushing. At some point, your strength fails, and the boulder runs you over. Then you have to go back down the hill and start again.

It doesn't have to be that way. It gets that way because, as you learned in Chapter 1, every force is conspiring to turn you into a commodity. Everything in this industry is pushing you to work harder for less money—but you don't have to let yourself get caught in that trap. Time blocking is your way out.

The irony is, real estate agents tend to be control freaks. They desperately want to control every aspect of a deal, especially the behavior of the buyer and seller. But all of that is outside of them, outside of their control. Their own time is one of the few things they *can* control, and it's the one thing they let run wild.

Why? It goes back to building block #2: Time Blocking. Your time is out of control because it's run by your feelings. What you need to do is uncomfortable, so you do what you feel like doing instead. Time blocking and focusing on the six building blocks is scary because it forces you to say no to things. So instead, you chase deals and put out fires, which makes you feel productive, even though it doesn't contribute at all to your long-term success.

It's time to stop. Take charge of what's actually yours to control—your time. Use it to build a lasting business and reclaim your quality of life, not just chase false opportunities. I promise you, time blocking is the only way to reliably do this, and it's absolutely essential for the other five building blocks.

Yes, it's scary at first. Examine that fear, as you learned in Chapter 2. Do what your coach tells you, as you learned in Chapter 3. Let go of your resistance to this idea, as you learned in Chapter 4. Just do it—you'll thank me later, I promise.

6: CRM

aybe you can help me solve a mystery.

Let's take a look at the behavior of so-called top agents in the industry. In theory, they should be the best people to learn from. In most cases, the majority of an agent's business is repeat and referral—50 percent or more, and sometimes a lot more.

At the same time, they spend the majority of their time, energy, effort, and resources working on lead generation and conversion—that is, working with strangers. Most of them have a CRM—a client relationship management system—but only a very tiny percentage actually use it.

The leads they are chasing cost money, up to a 35 percent referral fee in some cases. On average, only 3 percent of purchased leads convert, and when you factor in the cost, the conversion rate goes down.

Most of these leads are buyer leads. If you do not respond instantly, someone else will. That means it's a full-on chase, a race to see who can get to them first. In essence, I have to drop everything I'm doing to run out and show property (often random properties) to someone who may or may not be qualified or motivated, and I have to go through this fire drill one hundred times to possibly secure two sales.

Here's the other option.

You put the people you know and have done business with into your CRM. You call everyone every ninety days, in the time block you have designated for it. When these people are ready to buy or sell, they raise their hand and let you know—and they pay your full fee instead of demanding a discount.

You don't have to compete for this business because you've established yourself as their trusted advisor. There is probably an 80 percent or greater chance they will buy or sell with you. You just need to make these calls each day.

Five hundred people in the database . . . four calls each per year . . . two thousand total calls . . . two hundred workdays . . . ten calls per day . . . and you sell approximately twenty-five homes.

Just by working your CRM each and every day!

So I ask you: Why would anyone chase after "leads" instead of working their CRM consistently?

This is a serious question I've asked my coaching clients many times, and there is no good answer—only excuses.

Your CRM is the most powerful business tool at your disposal. It's the key to building relationships and becoming the trusted advisor that your clients come back to again and again. It's how you stop trying to convince people of your value and start building trust. It's how you move from a transactional business model to a relational one. It's how you stop yourself from becoming a commodity.

In an interview I heard once, Bruce Springsteen described himself as being in a lifelong conversation with his audience. That's what you need to do with your clients over your thirty-plus-year career in real estate. The CRM is how you do it.

NOT A DUMPING GROUND

To understand how to use a CRM properly, let's go back to the days when it wasn't so easy to hoard thousands upon thousands of contacts. You've already heard the story of how I pounded the pavement in my first year in real estate. I was knocking on two hundred doors a day and calling every expired listing, generating lots of leads.

Those leads didn't become clients automatically. One conversation doesn't do the trick, especially if the person isn't ready to make a move for months or even years. I had to follow up with every single person I made contact with, and do it consistently.

I started with index cards labeled 1 to 31 for the days of the month, and I put each lead's name on a card, so I followed up with them once a month. I didn't just make calls; for each door lead, I also wrote a handwritten note. I was building relationships through regular conversations.

It quickly got to the point where there were too many index cards to keep track of and too many notes to write every day. So, I hired a computer programmer to write software that would allow me to do this digitally, which cost me about $10,000. At the time, this was cutting-edge—a few other agents were doing the same, but it wasn't common practice by any means.

Today, the CRM is at the core of any serious business. The software is much more powerful, easier to use, and cheaper than it was thirty years ago, and there are many different options. Most agents already have some version of it.

However, they're not using it to build relationships.

In three decades of coaching, it has become more and more obvious to me that real estate is a repeat and referral business. As mentioned earlier, the vast majority of top-producing agents get 50 percent or more of their business from repeat and referral clients, and this figure can reach 80 percent, 90 percent, or even higher. All those clients are coming to them, already primed to trust and collaborate, no convincing necessary.

Still, agents have a fascination with chasing after strangers. It's a paradox: most of the business (and the highest-quality business) comes from people they know . . . but they spend most of their time chasing people they don't know. I would bet money that you do the same.

Because of that, you neglect and misuse the most important tool in your business. From my experience, I would guess that 90 percent of agents have a CRM, only 10 percent are actively using it, and less than 1 percent truly use it the way it's designed to be used. It's not because it's difficult to use—it has just been misunderstood and positioned incorrectly.

Most agents use their CRM as a dumping ground. They just throw names in there—open house leads, cold leads, anybody—and at best, they send out a generic email blast every once in a while. It's like a garage filled with clutter. You never want to go in there because finding or doing anything feels like a terrible chore. So, you just dump contacts in there, then hope and pray someone might call you someday.

This is a huge unforced error. You're bringing leads in through the front door and letting them slip right out the back door because you're not following up consistently and building a relationship.

Remember, this is a relationship business. Cultivating relationships is your *job*. CRM technology helps you do that. Using your CRM isn't about contacting the masses on a large scale. It's about nurturing your connections with individual people. Every communication that goes through your CRM should help position you as a trusted advisor.

NO EXCUSES

Even though the technology is simple and easy to use, agents always make excuses.

"I can track this stuff in my head. I don't need a program."

No you can't. Not even close. Your intuition and memory are wildly insufficient for this task. A healthy CRM includes hundreds of people, all of whom need to be individually contacted on a regular basis. There's no way you'll remember who to call when, let alone what you talked about last time.

"I don't know enough people to justify bothering with it."

Not true. You probably know lots of people—you're just afraid to put them in your CRM and start reaching out to them. It makes you uncomfortable because on some level, you're afraid of being rejected. Every agent's secret fantasy is to do business with everyone they know without having to talk to anyone. Without a CRM telling you what to do in black and white, you just won't do it.

If your network really is small, you just need to add one name per day—one person in your life in some way that you can commit to building a relationship with. It could be anyone: someone from school, Mommy and Me, the local chamber of commerce, the gym, anything. In one year, you can add two hundred people. By year three, you could have five hundred or more—and that's enough for most agents.

If you truly don't know anyone and aren't willing to go out and meet people . . . get out of real estate. This business isn't the right one for you.

"I can't go back and reconnect with the people I've ignored—it's too awkward."

This is my favorite excuse. You go through an intense period of communication with an active client, and then the deal closes. You intend to follow up, but day one goes by and you're too busy . . . then day two goes by, busy again . . . then day three . . . and the next thing you know, it has been a week, and now it feels awkward. A week becomes a month, a year, a decade . . . and you never see them again just because you never made that first call.

You have to go back and call those people, no matter how long it's been. You imagine they're going to be annoyed or confused. You imagine they won't want to talk to you. You imagine they'll think you're the worst real estate agent in the world.

So, just say it: "You're never gonna guess who this is . . . it's the worst real estate agent in the world." (This is a little preview of Tactical Empathy, which we'll tackle in Chapter 8.) Nine times out of ten, the response is positive. With one little sentence, the relationship is rekindled.

Agents love to play a game with themselves. They look at their list of leads and see potential deals, which feels good. As long as they don't actually follow up with those leads, they can continue pretending there are deals coming down the pipeline. They don't want to find out if the leads are real or not, because what if they're not? It feels better to think you might have a lead than to know that you don't. Most agents prefer a "maybe" over a definite "no." This is what the hope game is all about.

But remember, feelings are expensive. They keep you from doing what needs to be done in your business—like following up with potential leads.

The CRM problem is pervasive. I see it over and over, no matter how long an agent has been in this business or how high their production is. In fact, the top producers are often the worst at leveraging their CRM.

I'll go into the CRM of someone who has been in the business for decades and find they have only a few dozen people classified as past clients and a few dozen more as sphere of influence. All the other people who *should* be in those groups are lost somewhere in the ten-thousand-plus ungrouped contacts. Meanwhile, there are hundreds of incomplete tasks and countless people overdue for outreach, and software has flagged a thousand contacts as high-probability prospects.

Now, most of their business is already repeat and referral, but they're doing it by feel. They reach out to past clients in a random, haphazard way because it seems easier than dealing with their mess of a CRM. Imagine what they could achieve if they actually nurtured relationships with all their past clients and sphere-of-influence contacts.

It would take less than ninety days to clean up a CRM like this, using the steps I outline below. Then, the agent could come in every day, open it up, and have a real plan of action.

There is always resistance. There is always something that will make you feel anxious and uncomfortable about this process. But failure to use your CRM properly is the source of a lot of *other* discomforts. It is the reason you're constantly stressed and working 24/7. It's why you're always chasing, desperate for another deal. You will never escape that cycle until you learn to leverage your CRM.

Bottom line: There is *no excuse* not to use your CRM the right way. If you don't, you're just shooting yourself in the foot. Like I said, you won't want to do this at first, just like you won't want to do any of the other five building blocks. It doesn't matter. This is what it takes to build a real estate business without constant stress and overwhelm. If you want that, do this.

THREE RULES FOR CRM MASTERY

There are three things you need to do with your CRM.

1. Get the Right People In

Who belongs in your CRM? The people you are committed to following up with *at least* once a quarter. That includes four groups, plus an optional fifth one.

1. **Active clients:** This includes buyers and sellers who are currently working with you—they have signed a listing agreement or buyer's agreement. A good agent will have ten to twenty names in this group at any given time.
2. **Leads:** They're not ready to commit to buying or selling today, but they will be soon—no more than a year out. This group changes all the time but usually has ten to twenty people on average.
3. **Past clients:** All the people you've ever done business with and want to continue to be in a relationship with. If they've moved out of the area, consider removing them. If you don't want to do business with them again, remove them. Ideally, you will end up with one hundred to five-hundred-plus people in this group.
4. **Sphere of influence:** People you know but haven't done business with. You believe that if they wanted to buy or sell in the future, it would be with you. This group also typically includes one hundred to five-hundred-plus people.
5. **Other agents (optional):** Include this group only if staying connected to other agents is part of your business plan. Only save agents you network with on a regular basis, not every agent you've ever met, and definitely not agents you don't know personally. I doubt you would have more than fifty agents in this group unless this is a dedicated part of your business-building strategy.

Each person should be in only *one* group at a time. Moving a person into a higher-activity group—like from sphere of influence to leads, or leads to active clients—is easy. It's when you move them to a lower-activity group—especially from active clients to past clients—that you have to pay extra attention.

This transition feels unnatural, and it's where so many relationships fall apart. When you're in the middle of a deal, you talk with your client almost every day for thirty to ninety days. That's an intense relationship. Then, the deal closes, and suddenly there's no reason to call them anymore.

This is why people get disconnected. You don't know how to interact, so you just don't interact at all. If you don't take extra care of that relationship in the first ninety days after closing, chances are you'll never speak to that person again.

So, here's your transition plan. Talk to the client on the day of closing to congratulate them and make sure everything went according to plan. Then, check in a week later, then two weeks later, then four weeks later, then eight weeks later. On these calls, you're just asking them how they are and making sure everything is okay. After that, you can put them on the same ninety-day cadence as all your other past clients.

Again, this ninety-day window when an active client transitions to a past client is pivotal. In fact, the first year after a sale really sets the tone for the relationship over the long run. If you can generate a referral in year one, chances are you will generate more referrals and repeat business over time. This is something you really want to pay attention to. Your "just bought" or "just sold" action plan needs to be well thought out, yet simple, and your CRM makes it automatic if you set it up the right way.

In addition to groups, you can use tags to sort your CRM contacts in a more flexible way. For example, you may want to be able to see a list of everyone who has referred business to you. So, you would make a #VIP tag and apply it to those people. You may also want to tag people by the year they did business with you (#2021, #2022, etc.). For agents, you can tag them by the geographic areas they serve. Don't go crazy with this—only create tags for things you need to search for.

If you already have a database full of contacts, clean it up. Go through every name, and if you don't know who they are or why they're in there, delete them. Get rid of all the false hope.

Agents hate to do this. They think, *What does it hurt to keep them in there and send them stuff? Maybe they'll call.* NO. Think about the garage analogy. If it's not clean and tidy, you don't even want to look in there. Similarly, if there's even *one* person in your CRM who you don't want to call, it can deter you from using your CRM at all.

So, look at every single name and ask yourself: Am I committed to calling this person every ninety days? If not, delete. If you're not sure, delete. It's better to have zero contacts than five thousand contacts you're never going to call.

2. Get Everyone on a Contact Plan

By putting someone in your CRM, you're making a commitment to build a lifelong relationship with them. That means picking up the phone and calling them at least every ninety days. This is the minimum level of relationship required.

And yes, I said calling, as in over the phone, with your voice, live. You can layer in other forms of contact (texting, social media, email, mail), but the phone call is mandatory.

I know what you're thinking: *People don't answer the phone anymore—they prefer text messages.* I promise you—I *promise* you—a text does not build a relationship like a call does. Creating an emotional connection requires a real-time conversation with real human voices. Trust me, I'm not some old man who can't keep up with the changing times. I coach dozens of agents every single day, and I see what works and what doesn't. If the person doesn't answer the phone, fine. Leave a voicemail. Send a text. But first, call.

Every ninety days is the minimum, and that applies to your past clients, sphere of influence, and other agents. Leads require more frequent follow-up, perhaps once a week to once a month, depending on each person's specific situation. Active clients require even more—at least once a week, and maybe as often as every day, depending on what's happening with them. You should also consider calling people on their birthdays, home anniversaries, or other special occasions.

The important thing is to set up automatic reminders for all of this. If you try to rely on your memory, you are going to forget someone, guaranteed. Things will blow up with your active clients, and you'll forget to follow up with leads. You'll get excited about a lead who is about to commit, and you'll forget to check in with an active client. You'll get wrapped up in all the urgent activity of clients and leads and forget about your past clients and sphere of influence entirely.

A good CRM will make it simple for you to create these automated reminders. I can't give you step-by-step instructions because each software platform is a little different. Just know that this function is the key to using your CRM right. Make sure you choose a platform that makes this easy so that the system can automatically spit out a list of people to call every day with no effort on your part.

Let me be clear: a contact plan is *not* a drip campaign. No one wants to be dripped on. No one wants to get a generic email. You may still send some mass emails for things like your annual market analysis, an invitation to a client event, or a client survey. But the personal phone call is still your most effective relationship-building tool.

3. Get Your Dashboard to Zero Every Day

So, you've effectively cleaned up your garage. It's no longer a dumping ground—it's perfectly organized. Everything is there for a reason, and you know exactly where to find it and what to do with it.

Now, you have to keep it that way. That means when you put people into it, you have to put them where they belong, with all the pertinent information. Most importantly, you have to clear your dashboard every day. Yes, every single day. In the hour you've blocked off for your CRM, make all the calls and complete all the tasks your CRM tells you to do.

Let's talk about those calls, especially the ones that aren't to your active clients. Active client calls are relatively easy—you probably have something specific to talk about, and you're probably not worried about being rejected by the person on the other end. (Unless you need to have a tough conversation, but we'll get to that in Chapter 8.)

No, I know you're more worried about calling leads, past clients, and people in your sphere of influence. You think: *They don't want to hear from me—they know why I'm calling.*

Guess what? You are NOT calling to talk about real estate. This is NOT a sales call. You are NOT chasing a deal—you don't do that anymore.

You are just calling to say, "Hi, how are you?"

That's it. Nothing more. Ask about their job, their family, their pets, their hobbies, anything but real estate. *What's new in your life? How is your new puppy doing? How was your trip to Mexico?*

Why would you do this? Because your job is to build relationships. The purpose of this call is not to get something out of the other person or convince them of anything. It's simply a check-in to maintain your relationship, no different from what you would do with a casual friend or neighbor.

If the conversation doesn't result in any business, that's fine. That wasn't the goal. If you keep calling every ninety days, one day it will. You won't even have to bring up the topic of real estate; when they're ready to talk about it, they'll ask you. They'll say, "Actually, we're thinking about moving . . . how is the market right now?" Or *they'll* call *you* the moment they decide to make a move.

These calls are how you become a trusted advisor. And who would a client rather do business with: a trusted advisor or a stranger? You know the answer.

Still, you'll be tempted to skip these calls. The problem is wanting instant gratification. *Why make the call if I know they're not going to do business today? I'll go chase after strangers instead.* But if I live in a $5 million home, why would I work with an agent I don't know just because I get a postcard or see a post on Instagram? That makes no sense.

The search for instant gratification is what kills the repeat and referral pipeline. Relationships take time; you have to sow and cultivate the seeds every day. That's how this business works.

Just do the math. With two hundred working days in a year and ten calls a day, that's two thousand calls a year. If you call each person four times a year, that's five hundred people you can keep up with in just one hour per day of CRM time.

That's why this is the most important time block of the day. Treat it like a listing appointment. You would never cancel a listing appointment just because you're busy or something comes up. Until you elevate your CRM time block to this status, you'll never do it. Again, this is the MOST important activity you can engage in.

REJECTION IS NOTHING TO FEAR

Your CRM is your personal coach, your business plan, and your daily to-do list—and it updates itself every day. This is so much more effective than some annual plan you stick in a drawer. All you need to do is what your CRM tells you to do every day: call these people, send these emails.

Once agents understand this, the biggest roadblock is fear of rejection.

For example, one of my coaching clients works in Palm Desert. It's a second home community for a lot of people, especially from Canada. Buying a second home far away is a long process. People don't usually buy immediately—they come and rent for a year or two before deciding to buy.

This agent worked extremely hard to generate lots of business from online leads, and he spent a lot of time showing property to strangers. Over the years, he did a lot of deals and built up a rich database of potential sellers . . . but he didn't use it. He thought no one ever wanted to hear from him, so he kept chasing online leads.

Finally, one day I said, "Enough is enough. Call every single person in your database over the next ninety days."

He imagined every terrible response: people not remembering him, doing business without him, hanging up on him, yelling at him. In the deepest part of his mind, all those invented stories of rejection led to failure, poverty, and in the end, death. So, he kept avoiding that task.

I finally embarrassed him to the point that he started making the calls. All the negative things he imagined actually did happen . . . but he didn't die. And some people actually wanted to talk to him. In fact, he got business from doing it! Plus, he cleaned his CRM of the contacts who were never going to do business with him, so he had a clear picture of his actual network.

Remember, you are NOT calling to do business. You're just calling to say hello and have a quick chat. It's easy. If you're a people person, as most agents are, it should be the funnest part of your day. Don't psych yourself out by making this more than it is.

When you feel that fear telling you not to call—warning you that you'll be rejected—embrace it, examine it, and let it go. Just make the call. The more calls you make, the more evidence you'll have that they're not going to kill you, and the easier it will get.

■ ■ ■

We all have our own personal programming around relationships. If you're very lucky, yours is perfectly healthy, but most of us have our fair share of baggage. Whatever your fears, patterns, and habits are around relationships, they're deeply ingrained in your subconscious.

Unfortunately, your subconscious mind is a thousand times stronger than your conscious mind. You won't be able to think your way out of your current habits. The only way to change a habit is to . . . well, change the habit. Choose a different behavior, and do it many, many times, until the new behavior becomes the subconscious pattern.

If you use it right, your CRM makes that choice as easy as possible. You don't have to think at all—just look at your to-do list and do it, every day. There's no room to ask why or what if. Just make the calls. That's how you change your programming. Without this powerful tool, you'll stay stuck in your current patterns and never build the relationships that will power your business.

That's why, of all the work activities you could time block, your CRM is the only one I consider absolutely mandatory. You *must* spend one hour a day on this. There are a hundred other ways you can "get in front of people" or "stay in touch" with ads or mailers or newsletters or social media posts. None of that is essential. This is. Calling people is *by far* the most effective way to become their trusted advisor, and the trusted advisor is always the Favorite.

7: PROCESS **MANAGEMENT**

I n the NFL, when you go to training camp every year, the first thing they give you is the playbook. It has everything you need to know as a member of the team, from actual on-the-field plays to training regimens to rules and expectations about personal conduct. *Nothing* is missing. You have to know the playbook inside and out, and if you're asked to leave, you have to give it back.

As a real estate agent, you think you don't need a playbook for yourself. You believe you can just keep all the information about how to run your business in your head. *I know what to do,* you think. *I don't need a manual.*

Stop BS-ing yourself. You can't remember it all—that's why you find yourself running fire drills all the time. You're forever reacting to unexpected problems and scrambling to cover mistakes precisely because your business processes aren't written down.

By processes, I mean all the workflows in your business. That includes every single task you need to complete to keep the ship running, from internal work, like reviewing your finances, to client-facing work, like listing property, working with buyers, opening escrows, and closing deals. Creating a process means defining each step in that work flow, documenting it, and ideally, putting it into a cloud-based project management program (like

Monday.com, Asana, or one of the many others). That way, you can not only keep track of everything you do but also refine your processes over time.

Putting together a listing presentation is a great example of this. If you get a call from a potential seller requesting an interview, organizing your presentation should be a simple process. In real life, you know it's not. It's as if you've never done a presentation before, a mad dash to get it done as you're running out the door, with no time to review the materials. That's how agents arrive at listing appointments with wrong or incomplete information. Hopefully, this has never happened to you—it certainly never should.

It may feel unnatural to write down every step of your work, but this is not up for debate. Like all of the six building blocks, you *must* do this. I'm not saying this on a whim—after three decades of coaching agents like you, this is what I know to be absolutely essential for success. I guarantee, lack of process is putting an invisible ceiling on your business and your quality of life. Without it, everything is slower, less effective, and more stressful than it should be.

So, let's fix that.

THREE REASONS TO LOVE PROCESS

Processes make your business and life better in three key ways.

1. Processes Create Excellent Client Experiences

When you write down your best practices and follow them consistently, you minimize errors and maximize consistency. You can stay calm, think ahead, and have a strategic plan for each property. You can prepare your clients for what's coming around the corner so they have the right expectations and understand what problems may arise. And, of course, you'll be far less likely to drop any balls.

It's difficult to overstate the power of this shift. When you're calm, the client is calm. When you lay out the strategy and the possible pitfalls, they see that you know what you're doing and have a plan, which builds their trust in you. When you set expectations proactively, it prevents the misunderstandings that so often lead to disappointment.

The result is not only a smoother sale or purchase but also a smoother emotional experience, which is even more important. For the client, the actual deal is only part of what contributes to their satisfaction. In fact, what sticks with them more than the deal itself is how they *feel* about the deal. If they can get to the same outcome in a state of constant anxiety or in a state of calm confidence, which do you think they prefer? Which do you think will get you referrals and repeat business? You know the answer. Process is what makes that possible.

2. Processes Increase Your Quality of Life

Without it, real estate is *stressful*. There's so much to keep track of and so many people asking for your attention, all the time. If you don't have a clear guide to keep your priorities straight and make sure nothing falls through the cracks, guess what? Things will fall through the cracks. And then you're scrambling, and people are upset at you, and the stress just builds and builds—as do the demands on your time.

Wouldn't it be nice to avoid that mess? When you have processes to rely on, you'll avoid making mistakes and missing crucial steps, which means you'll have fewer reasons to panic, and other people will have fewer reasons to nag, doubt, or blame you. You'll also relieve yourself of having to mentally track everything you're supposed to do, which is a source of stress all by itself. With the right processes, you don't have to lie awake at night running through your mental checklists, hoping you haven't forgotten something. It's all right there, in your project management system.

3. Processes Make Your Business Scalable

If you want to grow, either as a solo agent or as a team, process is the first prerequisite. It's what allows you to maximize your efficiency so you can sell more without working harder. Even more importantly, it enables you to delegate responsibilities to others—even if it's just one assistant—so you don't have to do everything yourself. Without it, you only have chaos, and you can't scale chaos.

A BUSINESS, NOT A JOB

If processes are so great, why do most agents not use them?

Because they treat real estate as a job, not a business—whether they realize it or not. The difference is that a job is based on one person; take away that person, and there's nothing of value left. In a job, you earn income, but you don't build equity. You bust your butt for thirty years, and then your last deal is your last paycheck.

A business is bigger than one person, even if it's run by a solopreneur. It can grow to include other people and even be sold. It can continue generating value even without its creator. This is done in other industries all the time. If a doctor or lawyer can sell their business, why shouldn't a real estate agent? The reason this is so rare is the same reason agents neglect process: they treat this as a job, not a business.

I told you from the very start, this book is about building a business—specifically, a repeat and referral business. So, how do you start treating your work like a business?

Agents get stuck in "job" mode because they love to rely on their personality to get things done. They woo prospects with their charm, win them over with their powers of persuasion, and tap dance through the rest, putting on a show to keep clients happy while they rush feverishly behind the scenes to get the work done. It's a reactive and highly stressful way of operating, but it's what most agents are comfortable with because it's what they know. They believe their big, friendly personalities are the key to their success.

Solo agents can get away with it, sort of. In doing so, they take on far more stress than necessary and miss out on more business than they can ever know, but still, they can survive.

Teams can't. The moment a personality-driven agent starts to hire people, the chaos multiplies. Without processes to guide them, everyone has to just guess at what to do, when, and how—and they inevitably come to conflicting conclusions. Nothing is coordinated, mistakes keep happening, and everyone gets frustrated. That leads to high turnover, which only adds to the mess. This is why most real estate teams implode pretty quickly.

Process is the opposite of personality. It's orderly. It's predictable. It's repeatable. It doesn't care who does the task, as long as the task gets done right, and on time.

So, what I'm asking you to do is more than just write things down. It's a mindset shift, from personality to process. Your charisma is nice to have, but it's not the engine of your business. That honor belongs to your playbook—your processes. Even if you never intend to hire a single other person or sell your business, this is still the only way to build and grow a stress-free real estate business.

I won't lie—building processes is tedious work. If you're like most agents, you're a natural salesperson, not a systems person. The idea of documenting everything is like nails on a chalkboard; it's just not the way your mind thinks.

That's why everyone wants to skip this. But as you know by now, you don't succeed in life by avoiding the things that make you uncomfortable. To live a fulfilling life, you have to do a lot of things you don't want to do.

That said, you may be surprised. As soon as you sit down to think about how you do things, you'll probably find better ways that benefit you immediately. The more processes you nail down, the smoother your business will operate, and the less stress you'll have—and the more you feel these benefits, the easier it will be to do the process work.

ONE PROCESS AT A TIME

A process is not a complicated thing. You don't need any special skills or training to do this. At its heart, any process is a combination of three things you're very familiar with: instructions, checklists, and calendars.

For example, let's look at the process of holding an open house. You would need to plan out the following tasks:

- Preparing the house for viewing
- Promoting the open house
- Preparing everything you need to bring, including marketing collateral
- Collecting information from visitors
- Conducting tours of the property
- Opening and closing the home
- Following up with the seller
- Following up with prospective buyers

If you make a checklist for each of these steps and put them on the calendar ahead of time, you never have to think about what to do. You just look at your calendar and do what it says, and you'll know you have everything covered. Every time you do it, you adjust the process as needed, and after five or ten repetitions, it will be dialed in perfectly.

Modern project management software makes this easier to manage than ever. You can create one project template for sellers and another for buyers, including everything that goes into serving each type of client. Then, when you get a new client, you copy that template, put their name on it, and voilà—everything you need to track and manage that client is ready to go. And with a project set up for each client, you can easily see what has been done and what needs to be done across the board.

Eventually, you need to have a documented process for all the workflows in your business. Here's a basic list of what that would include. It's not meant to be exhaustive, but it's a great starting point.

- CRM
- Leads
- Buyers
- Sellers
- Transactions
- Marketing
- Finances
- Client Communication
- Customer Service

Don't expect to do this overnight. It will take time. If you aim to make just one checklist per week, within a year, you'll have at least forty, and that's significant progress.

The biggest struggle here is time. Agents hate to set aside time for anything that's not directly related to sales. This is where time blocking comes in—if you're going to do this yourself, block out at least an hour every week to work on it.

If you really struggle to think in terms of process, you may want to delegate this responsibility to someone with that skill. In fact, process management should be the main job of your assistant, if you have one. They're the ones who organize your workflow, so systematic thinking is the most important skill for that role. Don't worry about real estate experience—you can teach real estate. You can't teach someone to be systematic, especially if you aren't systematic yourself.

For example, a new coaching client of mine wanted to build a team—a true team, not just a mini brokerage (which is what most real estate "teams" are; more on that in Chapter 11). His very first hire was an operations person. Instead of hiring someone with real estate experience, he chose someone with advanced project management experience in another industry. Together, they have identified all the workflows that need to be defined, and the goal is to get them all done in a year. The result will be a team playbook.

Even when your business playbook is complete, your process management work is not done. It never is. Processes can always be refined and perfected, and they will have to evolve as the world around you changes. Every time you make a mistake or discover a better way to do something, it's an opportunity to improve your processes.

In football, we did that learning every week when we looked back at the film from the previous game. You should do the same after every deal. Look back and ask yourself what worked, what didn't, and what to add, remove, or change.

In fact, whenever anything goes wrong, look at the process first. No matter who made the mistake, chances are there is something you can improve in your process to prevent the same kind of problem from happening again. When you constantly evaluate your processes, you'll get better and better over time.

Just take one agent I coach, who throws a holiday party every year. It was more work the first year, with one hundred guests, than it is now for over five hundred people. That's because the process has been refined over the years. She knows exactly what to do and when; all she has to do is follow the checklist. It's easy.

■ ■ ■

Remember what you learned in Chapter 5: the reason real estate agents work seven days a week is because they don't work five. That is, they spend most of their time on the wrong stuff, so they never have time for the important stuff.

Lack of process creates a similar vicious cycle. The more inefficient you are, the more you have to work, and the more you have to work, the more inefficient you'll be—because you'll never take the time to create the processes that will make you efficient.

It makes no difference whether you're a team of one or fifty. You're building a business, and a real business can't rely on personality. Personality isn't transferable or scalable. It doesn't build equity. It doesn't make you better over time.

Process does.

It's just like the difference between amateur and professional sports. Amateurs rely on talent. Professionals have talent, but they don't rely on it to win. They think systematically about the best way to do things, and they constantly look for ways to do them better. Focusing on process will help you leave the amateur ways behind and act like a true pro.

If you would like to see some sample checklists, check out the book website at www.performancecoachingbooks.com.

8: TACTICAL **EMPATHY**

magine you're a hostage negotiator. When you walk into an active hostage situation, you're facing someone with demands—they want money, freedom, power, resources. They honestly believe it's a real possibility that those demands might be met. After all, they have leverage because you don't want them to hurt or kill the hostage.

You know better. There's no way this person is getting what they want. The only two possible outcomes for them are prison or death. That's reality. No one is going to just pay the ransom and let them go live their fantasy life.

As Brandon Voss puts it, your job is to sell them jail time.[2] That's hard to do—they're in a highly emotional state, with completely unrealistic expectations. They didn't start their day thinking, *I want to go to jail*, but that's exactly what you have to get them to do.

Real estate isn't *that* tough, but it's close.

You learned it in Chapter 1: hopes and dreams are on the line, and these hopes and dreams are *not* based in reality. Every seller

---

2   Son and business partner of Chris Voss, who is a former FBI hostage negotiator, author of *Never Split the Difference*, and my coauthor on *The Full Fee Agent*.

thinks their home is worth more than it is. Every buyer wants their perfect home for half of what it really costs. They don't know the world of real estate, just like the hostage taker doesn't know the world of military or police operations. They don't know their expectations are out of line, and they're already emotionally invested in them.

So, your job is to sell reality, and it's hard. Reality is so much worse than what they were hoping for. How do you get them to accept it?

Most agents just hammer people with facts, logic, and reason. It's a brute force approach, where the goal is to get the client to do something they don't want to do. You're *convincing* them to reduce their target price or compromise their buying criteria.

But you can't overcome emotion with facts, logic, and reason. And make no mistake, emotions are running high. This is probably the biggest financial decision they've ever made, and their choice affects their daily life in the most intimate, all-encompassing way. Plus, as any marketing expert will tell you, people don't buy rationally. They buy with their emotions and justify their choice afterward with facts, logic, and reason. So it's no wonder that a logic-based sales approach doesn't work very well in real estate.

This chapter will teach you a much better way: Tactical Empathy.

It's the art of influencing others by articulating what they're thinking and feeling, without necessarily agreeing, disagreeing, or sympathizing. It's not about taking their side or feeling what they're feeling. It's about making them *feel understood*.

If you've read my book with Chris Voss, *The Full Fee Agent*, this will sound very familiar. That whole book is dedicated to mastering Tactical Empathy. This chapter is a distillation of the essentials, which are crucial for building a stress-free repeat and referral business.

FIRST, CROSS THE ROAD

No real estate agent gets trained to make people feel understood. In all the real estate training you've ever done, there has probably been little to no mention of emotion at all, let alone empathy.

Instead, you're taught to believe that you get business by convincing people of your value. That's what the listing presentation is all about, right? It's you explaining the tangible benefits you'll give your clients in exchange for their money. Facts, logic, and reason.

Some agents get great at convincing, it's true. Maybe you're one of them. Maybe you think your presentation is pretty damn good—hey, it probably is. It doesn't matter. No matter how great it is, no presentation based on facts, logic, and reason is in alignment with how people really make decisions.

Until you engage with people's emotions, all your explanations fall on deaf ears. If they don't feel that you understand them—their situation, their needs, their perspective—they are *not even listening*. Maybe you do understand them, or at least, you think you do. Unfortunately, it doesn't count for anything unless *they* think you do.

Think of it this way. Imagine you're standing across the road from the other person. Usually, you shout and gesticulate wildly to get them to come over to your side so you can then lead them on the path you know they need . . . but they don't want to cross. It's a huge struggle to convince them. If they do come, it feels like you're dragging them the whole way—not a good experience for you, or for them.

Instead, you need to cross the road first. Go to them, stand by their side, and look at the world from their perspective. When they know you're seeing what they're seeing, *then* you can show them the various paths, help them choose the right one, and guide them along it. Instead of feeling pushed and manipulated, they feel supported and in control.

That's Tactical Empathy.

FIVE STEPS TO TACTICAL EMPATHY

To practice Tactical Empathy, there are five things you must do in every single conversation. Note that this isn't just for clients. Tactical Empathy can be used with everyone: your assistant, your vendors, other agents, your family, your neighbors, your friends. In every context, it creates the foundation for a productive conversation and a strong relationship.

1. Put Your Thoughts, Feelings, Desires, and Agenda on the Back Burner

This goes back to building block #1: A Mindset of Harmony. You've lived most of your life immersed in your preferences. You bring them to every situation, evaluating every moment based on whether it does or doesn't line up with what you want. If it does, you cling, and if it doesn't, you resist. You're always wrapped up in your own emotional situation, which leaves no space to attend to other people's emotions.

No more—now it's about them, always. Not you. Without this shift, empathy is impossible because empathy has nothing to do with your feelings and everything to do with theirs. If you've been practicing a Mindset of Harmony, you should be able to consciously set aside your preferences and approach the conversation with a truly open mindset, ready to listen fully to the other person.

2. Let Them Fully Express Themselves

Whatever they're thinking and feeling, encourage it to come out. The idea is for them to express themselves as fully as possible. There are a few key tools for achieving this.

One is labeling: taking an educated guess at what they're thinking and feeling, and saying it. "It sounds like you're frustrated." "It seems like you want to move quickly on this." If you're right, they'll confirm it. If not, they'll correct you. Either way, you find out what's on their mind.

You can even intentionally mislabel—say the *opposite* of what they seem to be thinking or feeling. This is especially effective when the person seems reluctant to open up. People hate to be misunderstood, so they will jump to correct you, often revealing more than if you labeled them correctly.

Another useful tool is mirroring: simply repeating the last few words they said. When people hear this, the natural tendency is to expand—to say more, take the train of thought further, and clarify what they mean. The more they say, the better you can truly understand their perspective.

3. Make Them Feel Understood

How do you know when someone feels understood? They say, "That's right." As in, "Yes, you get what I'm saying."

How do you get them to say that? Keep labeling and mirroring until you get a thorough view of what they're thinking and feeling. Then, summarize it for them. "It seems like what you're saying is . . ." and fill in the blank. If you were listening in Step 2, you'll hit the nail on the head, and they'll respond with, "That's right."

4. Help Them Think in Terms of Reality

No telling, selling, or explaining of any kind. Your job is not to present reality to them—it's to help them discover reality for themselves. That's the only way they'll believe it's true. It's also the only way to avoid being the one to blame for crushing their unrealistic hopes and dreams.

So, how do you guide them to discover reality? Use calibrated questions. These are "how" and "what" questions that make them think about solving the problems in front of them. "How should we proceed?" "What criteria are most important to you?" "What would need to happen to achieve that?" "How will you decide?"

It may sound almost like you're asking them to do your work for you. You're not—remember, you don't control other people. You can't make anybody do anything. They have to make all the decisions themselves, and you can only guide and advise them.

Plus, people love being asked what they think. It's deferential; it shows your respect for them, and it demonstrates that you're not trying to take away their control over their own lives. You are not a threat—you're just there to help. They're in the driver's seat.

Most importantly, these questions force them to confront reality. In answering them, they will begin to see that their expectations are unrealistic and that they'll need to make tough choices in order to move forward.

5. Move Forward or Exit Gracefully

After working through Steps 1 through 4, if the client is ready to move forward, simply ask, "How would you like to proceed?" They will outline what comes next, and you are now ready to put a plan in motion. Collaboration, not convincing, is key. This is not you telling them what to do. This is you guiding and then defining next steps so everyone is in agreement, on the same page, and moving forward with clear expectations and a path to follow.

Otherwise, understand that you can't help people who don't want to be helped. Instead, you must have the courage to walk away when someone is not willing to engage in a realistic plan of action. You are a real estate agent, not a magician.

In hostage situations, 93 percent of negotiations are successful. The other 7 percent of hostage takers come for suicide by police.

They are never going to cooperate, and nothing anybody could say or do is going to change that.

In real estate, there will always be some people who refuse to accept reality. They will insist on their unrealistic expectations, and they will demonize you for suggesting they can't get everything they want. You can't help these people, and you shouldn't try. If the other person can't have a conversation grounded in reality, it's time to exit gracefully.

This is never about making them wrong. Maybe they need more time to process things, or maybe they need to collide with the brick wall of reality before they'll accept it. Either way, you always want to leave the door open for them to come back to you if and when they let go of their unrealistic expectations.

So, don't try to be right. Just say, "It sounds like you already have a few good agents to choose from. Why don't you meet with them, and if none of them work out, you can always reach out to me again."

Throughout these five steps, the key is to *not be attached* to the outcome. The moment you're attached in any way, you lose the ability to be empathetic because being attached means that your preferences have taken center stage again. It negates the first step, which makes the rest of the steps impossible.

That's why these five steps are not always a simple, linear process. At any point, your own thoughts and feelings might enter the mix, and then you'll have to loop back to step one before you can continue. The stronger you are with building block #1, A Mindset of Harmony, the more effective you can be with Tactical Empathy.

APPLYING THE FRAMEWORK

The five steps you've just learned are a framework that can be applied in many situations in real estate. Now I want to walk you through six of the most important Tactical Empathy principles and how they play out in your business.

The Favorite or the Fool

First, let's go back to the idea of the Favorite or the Fool, which I brought up at the beginning of Chapter 1. As I said then (and again in this chapter), you've been programmed to believe that you get business by convincing someone of your value, and that your main tool for doing this is your presentation. You think that when you walk in the room to do your spiel, the prospect has an open mind.

Not true. At least 80 percent of the time, you get business because the client determined you were the Favorite before they even spoke to you.

There's no such thing as an open mind. Everyone has biases. Everyone has a past. Everyone has preferences. Even before they start looking for a real estate agent, the client has their own personal criteria of what a good real estate agent should be like. When they decide they need one, they start the search by asking their network for recommendations, looking around the neighborhood for signs, or searching online. Your name comes up, so they check out your website and your online reviews as well as those of some of your competitors.

Already, they've developed a strong idea of who they like the most, and they'll probably call that person first. But even if they know that person is the Favorite, they'll call the others too.

Why? Because they *think* they have an open mind. They want to believe they're giving everyone a fair chance. They believe someone might say something to change their mind. And after all, it's only responsible to do their due diligence and make sure they're not missing anything.

In reality, though, they don't have an open mind. Even if a potential seller is interviewing three complete strangers, the playing field is still not level. The potential seller always has a preconceived notion of what they like prior to starting this process, based on their past life experiences. They already have a Favorite, and the rest are Fools, just serving to give them free information and make them more confident in their top choice.

Every agent wants to assume the playing field is level—who doesn't want to believe they have a fair shot?—but that assumption is *always* wrong. Someone is the Favorite, and everyone else is the Fool in the game. Usually, if you don't know you're the Favorite . . . well, you're probably the Fool. And if you are not aware of this dynamic, you're likely to blindly spend hours preparing and doing your song and dance, hoping they'll pick you.

In most cases, you'll end up rejected for no apparent reason. How many times has this happened to you in your career? In your mind, you did everything right, but the business went to someone else anyway. How frustrating is that?

You're left asking for feedback: "What could I have done better?" To add insult to injury, the prospect tells you what you did "wrong." In truth, you didn't do anything wrong. You never had a shot to begin with. And all that effort was simply an exercise in futility fueled, once again, by hope. STOP IT!

Sometimes, you dig yourself into an even deeper hole. When you sense rejection is coming, you make a desperate attempt to prevent it by discounting your commission, offering to pay for staging, or making false promises about the value of the home. You sell a little piece of your soul, hoping to edge out the Favorite. Most of the time, it doesn't work, and you're left feeling like even more of a loser.

Occasionally, it does work . . . sort of. You're still the Fool, but you get hired anyway. Unfortunately, the relationship is off to a terrible start because you've made yourself a commodity by promising to work harder for less. That doesn't inspire trust and collaboration; it just invites the client to milk you for all you're worth, which means untold stress for you and a poor experience for the client. Once again, STOP IT! Don't do that to yourself.

So if the Favorite has already been chosen before the client calls you, the goal of the conversation isn't to win them over. That's impossible—their mind is no longer open. The only thing you can do is *find out* if you're the Favorite or the Fool. If you know you're the Fool, you can save hours of your precious time by choosing not to pursue a client you're never going to get.

All this begs the question: If you can't become the Favorite through your powers of persuasion, how do you do it?

Go back to building block #3: CRM. You're the Favorite when you've cultivated a relationship and positioned yourself as the trusted advisor over time, either with the prospect directly or with someone the prospect knows. That's why we're focused on building a repeat and referral business—because with repeat and referral clients, you're *always* the Favorite. That's the whole point of this book: to stop chasing deals and start building relationships from day one.

So let's ask another obvious question: How do you determine whether you are the Favorite or the Fool? You need to get proof of life.

Proof of Life

This comes right out of Hostage Negotiating 101. In a hostage situation, the first thing a negotiator needs is proof that the hostage is alive because if not, there's no real possibility of a deal. Same for you. Your first task is to find out if there's real potential for a deal *with you*—not just whether they're serious about buying or selling but also whether they're genuinely considering hiring you.

Proof of Life revolves around one question: "Why me?"

Tone and pace are critical. Low and slow. "I am curious . . . of all the agents you might know, what compelled you to call me?"

Listen very closely. You're looking for a robust response to this question. The potential client is going to share how they perceive your value. It's their opportunity to "defend" their choice to call you. In your mind, you want to figure out if they're just calling agents or if they called *you* specifically. When you listen intently, you will hear the difference.

If you're the Favorite, they are going to be very specific in their answer. They'll say things like:

"We looked at your website and loved the way you present and market your homes particularly . . ."

"We read all your Zillow reviews. We loved how people talked about . . ."

"Our best friend raved about the experience they had with you in selling their home . . . they shared how responsive and detailed you were in your strategy and approach . . ."

"We visited several of your home houses and observed how you interacted with the people coming in . . ."

In contrast, you might get a vague answer like:

"We were driving around the other day and saw one of your signs . . ."

"We received your postcard in the mail . . ."

"We did a Google search, and your name came up . . ."

The more generic the response, the greater the chance you are the Fool in the game.

And if you get the classic, "Why don't you tell me why I should hire you?" red flags should be going off.

When you're the Favorite, they will tell you. There is no reason for anyone to withhold or hide this from you. When you're the Fool, they'll want to seduce you or manipulate you because they want something from you—*free consulting*.

The Proof of Life concept is designed to get you to the truth in the most authentic way possible. No one has to pretend anything. As a result of embracing this concept, my top coaching clients no longer go on traditional listing appointments. Instead, they do a prelisting video call, no more than fifteen to thirty minutes in length.

They simply say: "I would love to come out to your home. If you're not opposed, could we first set up a fifteen- to thirty-minute video call where you can tell me more about your situation?"

If they resist the video call in any way, you may be the Fool in the game.

Once you get on the call, start the conversation with a straightforward question, such as, "If you don't mind, please tell me what is going on?"

Again, more clues. The more open they are, the better. If they seem guarded, you may be the Fool. Use the five-step framework you just learned to make them feel understood and see if they're willing to have a conversation based in reality.

Once they have fully expressed themselves and you have paraphrased and summarized the situation so they feel understood, then comes the Proof of Life question: "Why me?"

And this is where you get to the truth . . . are you the Favorite or the Fool? You can figure it out in fifteen to thirty minutes or less. When you have a hunch about which it is, see if you can confirm it. If you sense that you're the Favorite, ask: "At the risk of being presumptuous, would it be wrong to assume we're going to be working together?" If you sense that you're the Fool, ask: "Would I be wrong to assume you're meeting with me as part of your due diligence, and you're probably leaning in a different direction in terms of the agent you want to work with?"

It sounds crazy, but it's surprisingly easy and effective. Either way, you'll find out the truth. If they want to work with you, they'll say so. They may ask questions or bring up objections, but only to make sure they're not missing anything or leaving any money on the table (e.g., "Is there any way you could do it for 5 percent?").

If they hesitate or attack you, you're the Fool. In particular, if they try to make you wrong or criticize the way you do business (e.g., "Everyone *else* charges 5 percent."), they're not serious about working with you. It's time to make a graceful exit.

If you're the Favorite, you set a plan for moving forward. If you're the Fool, you exit gracefully. Either way is okay. As Chris Voss likes to say, "It's not a sin to lose business. It's a sin to take a lot of time to lose business."

Listing presentations are a charade. All the prep time, the presentation time, the follow-up time . . . it's a full day or more of unpaid work, for nothing. Sellers know who they want going in. You don't need to interview for a job you are not going to be hired for. You don't need to do free consulting for someone who has no real intention of working with you.

With Tactical Empathy, you can streamline this process tremendously. You just need the courage to get to the truth and give up your fears and hopes, which lead you to wasting a lot of your valuable time.

Beware: you will be tempted to skip the Proof of Life step. A lead will come along, and maybe they'll seem like a sure thing right off the bat, or you'll be so hungry for clients that you don't care. You'll decide to forget about the video call and just do the listing appointment . . . and that's how you fall right back into the pattern of wasting your valuable time on low-probability activity.

For example, one of my clients got a phone call from a possible seller who had been referred by a neighbor. It was a strong referral. The initial conversation went something like this:

Seller: We are thinking about listing our home, and we were referred to you by our neighbors. They shared what a great experience and result they had with you.

Agent: Thank you.

Seller: We are going to be interviewing agents, and we wanted to find out if you were taking on new clients at this time.

Agent: Absolutely. I would love to help you.

Seller: We are extremely busy and would prefer to meet by video. We can do an in-person meeting if necessary.

Agent: Great. When can we set a time to meet in person? I would love to come see your home.

Most agents would do exactly the same thing my client did. In his mind, the referral from the neighbor was a real positive, and he figured if he could meet in person, he could increase his chances for getting the listing.

Let's rewind the tape and run this scenario through the Proof of Life filter:

- **Referral:** good.
- **Interviewing other agents:** given they had a strong referral and still wanted to interview other agents, maybe not so good.
- **Asking if he was still taking on clients:** a little guarded, not so good.
- **Very busy and wanting to meet by video:** sounds like due diligence to me.

There are some mixed signals here and definitely no clear Proof of Life yet. The agent could get that in fifteen minutes on a video call. Instead, he's going to spend four to eight hours on the preparation, presentation, and follow-up. Why? Most agents would rather live in hope over a prolonged period of time than get to the truth right away.

What about the idea that meeting the client in person increases your chance of getting hired? The basic premise behind that idea is that the force of your personality can overcome the biases and preferences they developed before they ever even called you. That's simply false 80 percent or more of the time. They already know what they want, and your charisma won't change that.

You will find yourself in circumstances like these all the time. You will have the opportunity to get to the truth in fifteen minutes, or you can settle for "maybe" and keep kicking the can down the road as long as possible, hoping to get the outcome you want. Your choice.

Get the Elephants Out Early

This is a phrase one of my coaching clients, Danielle Lazier, coined early on when Chris and I started teaching Tactical Empathy. "Get the elephants out early"—as in, the elephants in the room. The things no one wants to talk about that get in the way of everything else.

Most agents will do anything to avoid a tough conversation. They fear being disliked or being the target of someone else's negative emotions. Unfortunately, real estate is full of hard choices and unexpected problems that need to be talked about. To avoid the ugliness, agents love to put those conversations off, dance around them, or sugarcoat them . . . which only makes it worse. These tactics undermine trust because the other person can see you weren't upfront with them.

Tactical Empathy makes it easy to have those conversations by using an Accusations Audit™.[3] This is a tool designed to make it easier for the other person to take bad news. Whatever they may "accuse" you of, you say it first. Here's how it works.

First of all, don't wait. As soon as you know a tough conversation is needed, do this. The longer you put it off, the more it seems

---

3   Trademarked by Chris Voss, used with permission.

like you're trying to hide something, and the less time they have to deal with the problem.

Start by bracing them for what's coming: "I have some bad news." This alone makes a big difference—a sudden blow hits harder than one you've prepared for.

Then, label all the negative thoughts and feelings you imagine they might have—the more extreme, the better. "You're not going to like this." "You're going to be so disappointed." "You're going to think I'm the worst agent in the world." "You're going to want to fire me." "This is going to break your heart." These are the accusations: all the things you believe they'll accuse you of when they hear the news.

Say it all, and keep going until they ask you to stop and just tell them what's going on. Only then do you break the bad news. Inevitably, it will feel less bad than they thought it would, because you built up the expectation of pain. In most cases, they will thank you for being upfront and collaborate with you to move forward.

This sounds crazy, I know. It's probably the exact opposite of what you usually do, which is to put off the conversation as long as possible and then try to make the bad thing seem less bad than it really is. No more spinning. No more sugarcoating. No more editing. No more avoiding. Stop doing those things—they are killing your relationships. Try this instead.

Put the Responsibility Where It Belongs

Let's start with an example of something you deal with on a regular basis that often causes a lot of stress: inspections and requests for repair.

You know how hard it is to negotiate a deal and get someone under contract. Then you do inspections, which may lead to another round of negotiations. Think about what happens when the report shows a lot more issues than anticipated. Your buyer gets anxious. You get anxious. The other agent gets anxious. The seller gets anxious. Everyone is anxious. Am I wrong?

You have no control over the buyer or the other agent or the seller. However, you do have control over your own emotions and how you talk with your client in this situation. Here's an approach you've probably never tried:

Agent: Would I be wrong to think the report was a lot worse than you expected or were planning for?

Buyer: It was.

Agent: You are probably feeling some uncertainty about how you want to respond.

Buyer: We are.

Agent: Would you be opposed if I lay out a couple of different options?

Buyer: That would be great.

Agent: One option is to ask them to fix everything in the report and see how they respond, knowing the answer may be no.

Buyer: Okay.

Agent: The second option is to only ask for the things that are absolutely critical to you and nonnegotiable. Again, they may say no to this request also.

Buyer: What do you think?

Agent: You have to decide what you are most comfortable doing.

Buyer: You must have an opinion.

Agent: Option 2 is what has worked best for most of my clients. However, every situation is different. What is your gut telling you right now?

Buyer: Option 2 feels like the better decision.

Agent: What specifically would you like to request?

Buyer: _____, _____, and _____.

Agent: Are you sure?

Buyer: We are.

Agent: I will submit this and let you know when we get a response.

This is a very stripped-down version of what it sounds like to keep the responsibility where it belongs.

You don't need to be upset on your client's behalf. You don't need to tell anyone what to do. You don't need to have a perfect solution for everything—and to think that you should is both delusional and unhelpful. These behaviors are what happens when you're worried about looking good to the client, not about serving their best interests.

As we mentioned earlier in the book, every sales encounter starts off with you on one side of the street and your prospect or client on the other side. Without Tactical Empathy, you're shouting at them to cross the road and then dragging them down the path you "know" is right for them. That's taking a lot of responsibility for decisions that aren't yours to make and problems that aren't yours to solve—which is exactly what agents do all the time.

This is why you're so stressed so often. You're taking responsibility for things you have no control over. Remember, you do not control anything or anyone except yourself. You do not get to make any of the decisions in this process—you're not the one buying or selling a home. Deciding is the client's job. Yours is only to guide and advise.

Most agents, in the attempt to advise, actually end up trying to persuade the client to take whatever course of action the agent thinks is best. Whether the agent is "right" or not, the client feels pushed. They might give in to this push or resist it, but either way, it's not a good experience—anything that undermines their sense of control is an unwelcome threat.

Tactical Empathy turns this dynamic on its head. Not only can you advise in an effective way while allowing the client to feel in control, but you can also eliminate any potential stress or anxiety for both you and your client. Even in very tough situations, no one has to panic.

First, brace your client for what they are about to hear, as you learned in the last section. Then, lay out the facts of the situation—not your opinion of the facts but just the facts themselves. Let them know what they are up against.

Then, lay out their choices. Describe each alternative in terms of both potential gains *and* potential losses. The latter is especially important; people tend to overlook potential losses, and bringing these risks to their attention can dramatically change their view.

Once you've done that, use the five-step framework. Let them express themselves fully. Make them feel understood. Get them thinking in terms of reality.

Most importantly, keep the responsibility on the decision-maker. Don't let them put it back on you. The deal is going to happen or not—it's not your call to make. You are not attached to the result, so there is no burden for you to shoulder.

It doesn't mean you don't care. You advocate for your client at all times—that's your job—but you don't have to live in fear and hope to do that. This can be a no-drama zone. You can speak the truth in a way people can hear you. This is what it means to be trustworthy, competent, and a straight shooter.

End by asking what they want to do. Remember, they don't *need* to do anything. It's not your job to save them from themselves. What you want or think is best doesn't matter—it's about them, not you. You are the trusted advisor, not the persuader, and definitely not the decision-maker.

They may feel anxiety, frustration, or other negative emotions about what's happening. You don't have to share those emotions—

you just need to acknowledge them. Agents spend way too much energy taking on other people's feelings, believing that if they're not upset on the client's behalf, the client will think they don't care.

Not true. Your being upset doesn't help anyone—not your client, and not you. Just imagine being on an airplane and experiencing sudden, violent turbulence. You're terrified. Would you rather see the flight attendant terrified as well, or calm? Obviously you want a calm flight attendant—that reassures you that there's nothing to worry about and everything will be fine.

Again, this goes back to building block #1. Nothing is personal, not even the client's feelings about what you're telling them. It's not your place to take on their stress or make their decisions for them. The best way to support them is to stay calm, show them the landscape, and let them choose where to go.

Let Them Say No

Classic momentum sales tactics say you should aim to get people to say yes. Get to three yeses and you've made the sale, or something like that.

That's BS. No one wants to say yes—it makes them feel manipulated and vulnerable. They're not stupid; they know salespeople will push for a yes with questions that are designed to make them feel bad if they say no. So, they'll give you a fake yes just to see what you'll say next, but it doesn't mean they've gotten any closer to hiring you.

On the flip side, people love to say no—it makes them feel in control. It asserts their sovereignty. It's comfortable. And once they're comfortable, they're more open to listen to what comes next.

So, ask no-oriented questions. You're much more likely to get the result you're aiming for if the other person gets to say no. For example:

- Is this a good time to talk? → Is this a bad time to talk?
- Can I share a story? → Would you be opposed to me sharing a story?
- Can we do a Zoom call before I visit the property? → Would it be a bad idea to do a Zoom call before I visit the property?
- Would you be willing to stage the property before we list it? → Would it be impossible to stage the property before we list it?

These questions are exactly the same, except the answer that serves your purposes best is no instead of yes. You're putting yourself in alignment with what the other person already wants to say. Once they've said no, they're much more open to collaboration. Then you can start using calibrated questions (from Step 4 in the Tactical Empathy framework) to get them thinking in terms of reality and making decisions for themselves.

This is a completely different way of thinking. It's going to take time to get comfortable asking no-oriented questions. It's going to feel unnatural and awkward at first. Stay very conscious and deliberate until this new behavior becomes automatic.

People want to feel like it is their choice to do something. No one wants to be told what to do. No one wants to feel manipulated. When you give people the space to say no, they feel empowered, and it opens the door for them to do what you know needs to be done—and for you to find out whether or not they're truly willing to do it. This is a very easy skill to develop; it just takes a little patience on your part.

Think about it. What's your first instinct if someone says to you, "Would this be impossible?" Yes, it would be impossible, or no, it wouldn't? Try this in every situation you can, starting today. Would this be impossible? Would this be a bad idea? Would you be opposed? Would this be too much to ask? Would it be out of line? Would it be a terrible thing? Would I be imposing on you?

Again, people love to say no. Take full advantage of this human characteristic.

Nail the Lasting Impression

People always tell you to worry about the first impression. You only get one, right? But the same is true of the last impression, and when it comes to generating repeat and referral business, that's what matters most. People don't remember how things happened—they remember the most intense moment and how it ended.

That's why you should never split the difference to close a deal. It makes everyone feel like they lost a little, and that's the feeling they take away from the whole experience, even if it was good up until that point.

Instead, use the Tactical Empathy framework. Make them feel understood, help them think in terms of reality, and let them make and own the decision. Whatever they choose to do (even if it's to split the difference), they'll know it was the best way to get what they really wanted.

Remember, it's never about what you want. For example, one of my coaching clients has a long-standing relationship with one of his sellers. The seller referred a buyer to the agent, and the buyer ended up being interested in one of the seller's properties. There was no referral agreement in place, and the agent asked me how he could prevent the buyer and seller from simply working out a deal on their own, without him.

My advice? Let them do it. If the agent tries to force or convince them to work with him, they'll feel manipulated and won't trust him. Then, he'll lose their business forever as well as anyone they might have referred to him.

Instead, he should use Tactical Empathy: make them feel understood, lay out the options (to work with him or do the transaction directly), and let them choose. That establishes him as the trusted advisor who puts the clients' interests first, over his own financial interests. If the clients choose to walk away, they'll do it knowing they can trust him, and they'll go back to him when they need him. That's the lasting impression that will build your business.

PRACTICING TACTICAL EMPATHY

Tactical Empathy is a powerful tool. The catch is, you have to let go of everything you've done in the past. As you can see from this chapter, Tactical Empathy is often the polar opposite of what your instincts and habits tell you to do.

If you've been successful in the past, this will be very hard. Your habits don't want to die. They'll try to convince you that the devil you know is better than the devil you don't know. But I've been teaching this to my clients since 2017, and the evidence is overwhelming: Tactical Empathy dramatically increases your chances of success.

This isn't about scripting things out because they're unnatural. If you're truly focused on the other person, this *is* the natural way to think, speak, and act. This is how you give your highest and best to the moment, as you learned from building block #1.

Tactical Empathy just feels unnatural at first because it goes against what you've been programmed to do for so long. When I do live role-plays and put agents on the hot seat to practice Tactical Empathy, they do best when they're not really trying. It's when they start to think too hard that they stumble.

That's why you've got to get your reps in. Build up muscle memory. It's not complicated. You just need a low-stakes environment to practice in. Luckily, you can practice Tactical Empathy in virtually every conversation you have. As I said earlier, it applies to everyone, in any situation. The key is coachability: being committed to doing what you're told.

Once you work through the initial discomfort, the rewards are massive. Just imagine how many hours you'll save by not going on dead-end appointments . . . how much easier your tough conversations will be . . . how much stress you'll alleviate by not taking on your clients' emotions and responsibilities . . . and how much faster your business will grow when clients truly see you as a trusted advisor who puts their interests first.

Plus, there's a hidden benefit: you don't have to get rejected anymore. It's hard when you're putting your best foot forward and getting "no" for no real reason. That hurts. No wonder agents constantly question who they are and what they're doing. Once you understand what's really happening, you can avoid the vast majority of that rejection altogether.

You can also stop overpromising and giving discounts to get business. Every time you do that, you're selling a little piece of your soul, which adds up over thirty-plus years. That's what makes agents hard and jaded. Everything becomes about winning and losing.

That's not the way the world actually operates, and you don't have to operate that way either.

▩ ▩ ▩

This stuff is revolutionary: it completely changes the way you think, speak, and act. It's real, authentic, and impactful. You know why? Because this is a relationship business, and relationships are based on emotion, not fact, logic, and reason. They're based on trust, not value. Real estate isn't rocket science, but Tactical Empathy is rocket fuel for your business.

This either speaks to you or doesn't. I'm not here to convince you this is what you should do. But if this stuff isn't true, please explain to me why you go on appointments where you're the logical choice, and you nail the presentation . . . but you don't get the listing? I can't tell you how many times an agent has asked me, "What's wrong with my presentation? What am I doing wrong?"

There's nothing wrong with you. You just weren't the Favorite. There's no fact, logic, or reason about it. It's emotional.

In the end, this is about understanding the rules of the game. If you go out on a soccer field and try to play by the rules of football, you're going to fail. That's what you've been doing this whole time: trying to play the game of fact, logic, and reason on the field of emotion. When you learn the real rules, everything changes.

9: NUMBERS TRACKING

f I asked you right now what your year-to-date production is, could you tell me?

Nine out of ten agents can't. They're so busy chasing deals that they don't make time to find out what's really going on in their business. They don't know what they're earning, what they're spending, or where the business comes from.

So, they're making decisions every day based on instinct and impulse instead of fact. This is the part of your business you *don't* want to operate based on emotion. You need fact, logic, and reason—otherwise, you'll waste your time, energy, and money every day.

The biggest example is your commission. Why do agents think it's okay to charge 5 percent instead of 6 percent? Why do you give away your money so easily?

You think you can afford to because you're only looking at that one deal. It seems like a good decision to give up a few thousand dollars to get a deal. In reality, when you add up all the discounts at the end of your career, what you gave away was your retirement. You'll never understand that until you run the numbers and know your profit margin on each deal.

Bottom line: you can't know your business unless you know your numbers, and you can't leverage what you don't know. This final building block will solve that problem so you can make business decisions based on reality instead of wishful thinking. What gets measured gets improved, and managing your numbers will go a long way toward improving the health of your business.

WHERE DOES IT COME FROM?

Agents love to brag about sales volume and gross income. They plaster those numbers all over their marketing materials so everyone can see how "successful" they are. They obsess over how their numbers compare to others in their market and worry about how clients perceive their track record.

Unfortunately, those numbers don't mean much by themselves. You can sell a lot of homes and bring in big commissions but still go home with an empty pocket—or at least less than you expected. Unfortunately, agents tend to focus on the top line, not the bottom line, and they make poor financial choices as a result. Sales volume and gross income might be sexy, but they don't show the full picture and can give you a false sense of security.

The first question you need to answer is this: How much business are you *really* doing?

This starts with the number of transactions and closed sales volume, but it doesn't stop there. For each deal, you need to track your gross commission as well as the net commission, after paying your broker. That's simple enough: just multiply the gross commission by your split.

Then, you need to deduct your expenses to get the net profit before taxes. To get a quick-and-dirty estimate of what each transaction is costing you, just add up all your business expenses in the last twelve months and divide them by the number of transactions you did.[4] That's the average cost of each deal. Subtract that from the net commission of each deal to get your net profit before taxes.

That's *still* not your actual take-home income. To get that, you have to deduct taxes as well. To estimate your tax rate, just divide your total tax bill by the total taxable income from the most recent tax year. Multiply that rate by your net profit to get your taxes, then subtract your taxes from your net profit to get your net profit after tax. *That's* how much money you actually get to put in your pocket on each deal.

In summary, here are the numbers you should be looking at for each and every transaction:

Sale Price	What the home sold for
Gross Commission	Sale Price multiplied by Commission Rate
Net Commission	Gross Commission multiplied by Your Split
Net Profit Before Tax	Net Commission minus Expenses
Net Profit After Tax	Net Profit Before Tax multiplied by (1 − Expected Tax Rate)

Next, you need to know where your business is coming from.

The first question is, how much of your business comes from repeat clients and referrals? Many agents can guess at this, but they don't really know because they aren't actively tracking it. For most

---

4   Going forward, it would be smart to track the specific expenses related to each transaction so you can see the profitability of each one more accurately. To account for overhead (expenses that don't apply to a specific transaction), just divide your total annual overhead by the number of transactions in a year. Also note that if you're running expenses through your business that are really more personal than business, this makes it harder to get an accurate sense of your profitability.

established, successful agents, it's at least 50 percent, if not 70, 80, or even 90-plus percent.

The goal is to increase this number over time, ideally to 100 percent. As I've said before, repeat and referral business is better in every way. It's easier and less expensive to get, and the client is already predisposed to trust you. That makes collaboration easier, so they're more likely to get the outcome they want, have a good experience, and give you more repeat and referral business in the future. It's a virtuous cycle.

Beyond that, you also need to find your strategic sweet spot. If you look at the source (how the client found you), location, price point, and property type of all your transactions, you'll probably find that around 50 percent fit a similar profile. That profile is your sweet spot. The other 50 percent are all over the place—and most agents spend more time and resources reaching outside their sweet spot for deals than inside.

Ideally, you want to be doing *all* your business in your sweet spot. That's where you've developed deeper expertise and brand recognition, which is your competitive advantage. Instead of wasting your time pursuing deals outside of that zone—which you're less likely to actually get—double down on that competitive advantage.

For this, a traffic light analogy is useful. Anything in your sweet spot is green—that's what you should be looking for. Yellow opportunities are close to your sweet spot, but not quite in it. If they come along, go for it, but don't go seeking them out. Red opportunities have no relation to your sweet spot, so avoid them completely. They are a waste of time because they take more effort and do not contribute to growing your competitive advantage. All deals are not equal in value. Green deals are much more valuable than yellow or red deals.

This is another application of the inch-wide, mile-deep principle. Don't try to be everything to everyone. Identify your strengths and double down on them to create a specific competitive advantage.

This is not rocket science. When you use your CRM properly, it's easy to track where your business is coming from. Every deal should be recorded in your database and should include the source, location, price point, and property type. You just have to take the time to pull some reports and see what's there.

The goal is simple: to outperform yourself. Every year, you should see a higher percentage of repeat and referral business as well as a higher percentage of transactions in your sweet spot.

WHERE DOES IT GO?

Now, let's look at where your resources—both time and money—are going. Few agents track this, and as a result, they end up spending most of their resources on things that give them nothing in return, without even realizing it.

You should be spending your resources where you have a competitive advantage. The biggest competitive advantage is inside your database, with people who already know you. Out of all the people in the world, they are the most likely to trust you and want to do business with you. They're also the people most likely to pay your full fee. So, logically, you should be investing more resources there than in any other marketing efforts.

Most agents don't. They spend far more time on social media than in their CRM, trying to make "impressions" and get likes and comments from the whole world. That's no way to build relationships. It takes real, person-to-person, human-voice conversations to build the trust that will make people want to do business with you.

I know you don't want to hear this, but there is no contest between CRM and social media. There is only a select group of agents who have cracked the code of social media. It is not easy by any means, and even those who are successful with social media still need to make CRM a bigger priority. Once you do business with someone, you want to build that relationship into a source of repeat and referral business.

Agents also spend way too much time seeking out and doing business where they have no competitive advantage. Even the most dominant agents rarely have more than a 10–20 percent share of their main market—there's plenty more to capture there. Still, they insist on going out to the yellow and red zones, where they are less likely to win business, and if they do, it doesn't strengthen their competitive advantage. Everyone wants to go a mile wide and an inch deep, when going an inch wide and a mile deep is how you build a strong business.

So, you need to track both your time and your expenses closely. This is the only way to know what it actually costs to run your business and what you get for the resources you invest.

In particular, watch out for any spending that's not part of a coordinated strategy with a budget. This includes any one-off thing that you're just "trying out"—things like ads, mailings, lead generation, events, SEO, digital marketing, etc. If you haven't thought it through and made a commitment to doing it repeatedly, that's a red flag. If you're doing it to be smart or innovative, red flag. If you're doing it to get business tomorrow, red flag.

As I said in Chapter 1, real estate is a battle for consistency. That's what you get paid for—not smarts or innovation. It's a relationship business, and relationships are a long-term game. There's nothing you can do to get more business tomorrow. No instant gratification, no thirty-day ROI.

The point of all this is to align your time, energy, and money with where your business is actually coming from. All those resources are limited. You can't do everything. That's reality. Knowing that, you want to allocate your resources in the most effective way possible. If you're not paying attention, you'll end up spreading them too thin, with far too much invested in the things that don't matter and far too little in the things that do.

AVOID THE PITFALLS

To succeed at knowing your numbers, you'll need the help of the other building blocks.

In particular, building block #2 is crucial. If you don't block out time every month to review your numbers, it simply won't happen. And if you're not time blocking, you can't know how much time you spend on each deal, or on each of your work activities—so how can you know what your time is worth?

That knowledge makes a huge difference. When you understand what your time is worth, you won't waste it on work you can pay someone to do for much less. If you're worth $300 per hour as a salesperson, when you're doing work an assistant could do, you're losing $270 an hour. That changes things, doesn't it?

You also need building blocks #3 and #4. If you don't track your transaction data properly in your CRM, it won't happen. If you don't set up a process to make reviewing your numbers as easy and automatic as possible, it won't happen.

But of all the building blocks, #1 is the most critical for managing your numbers. That's because for most agents, mindset is the biggest obstacle. If you're afraid of what your numbers will reveal, you'll avoid looking at them. And if you're focused on instant gratification, you won't make time for this task because it doesn't make you money immediately. To manage your numbers, you have to *let go* of both of these things—your fear and your desire.

Beyond just analyzing your numbers, there's the challenge of actually changing them—bringing your spending of time and money into alignment with your strategic objectives. In this, there are three common beliefs that are guaranteed to get you off track.

"Something is better than nothing." This is a death sentence. It's what makes you compromise your standards and sell little pieces of your soul to get business, which is what puts you in a transactional orientation instead of a relational orientation with your clients. The moment you think this, you have turned yourself into a commodity. Can you survive this way? Yes, for a while. But it puts you on the path to inevitable burnout, where work has taken over your life and you resent every minute of it but feel like there's no escape.

Something is *not* better than nothing. How you do business matters more than how much business you do. Instead of chasing and desperately grasping at bad opportunities, let them go. That's the only way to make room for the good opportunities and the relationship work it takes to get them.

"I need results now." The desire for instant gratification makes you spend your time and money recklessly, without a strategy or plan. It's what makes you chase deals instead of working on the building blocks. It's what makes you buy ads, mailings, and other marketing services without a strategic plan. It's what makes you jump from idea to idea, wasting resources on shiny objects that won't do anything for you.

There are no instant results in this business, as I've said many times before. It's a long-term game, so don't let yourself pretend otherwise, ever. Even in the toughest times, the only thing that will save you is focusing on the six building blocks.

"I can make things happen." Again, this only serves to divert your attention from the fundamentals and pit your will against the universe. That's a battle you're never going to win. If you try, you're guaranteed to waste lots of precious time and money, not to mention generate plenty of stress and frustration. Your job is not to make things happen—it's only to be ready for when things do happen.

Virtually everyone in real estate is thinking these three things, all the time. That doesn't make it right. That's why building block #1 is so incredibly important for managing your resources. If you can't let go of your fears and desires, they will lead you on a spending spree that puts your time and money completely out of alignment with your goals.

■ ■ ■

If you can learn to manage your numbers, you'll be light years ahead of most real estate agents—even the "high performers." They love to brag about their closed sales volume, but what you don't see is all the wasteful spending and commission discounts it took to get there.

This is what I've learned from working with thousands of agents over thirty-plus years: even when agents look successful on the surface, if you strip down their businesses to the studs, they're miserable, they work 24/7, and they don't make as much money as you think. You don't want to put yourself in a situation where, after accounting for your expenses, you are actually netting a fraction of what you think you are.

This tells you that something is terribly wrong. Fortunately, it's all within your control. You choose how you spend your time and money. To make better choices, all you have to do is *pay attention*. Open your eyes. Watch where your resources are going. Make sure they line up with your strategy. And when they don't, change your spending habits. It's that simple.

PART III:
STAYING ON TRACK

10: DO YOUR JOB

"**D**o your job."

This may be the phrase I use more than any in my daily coaching practice. In the end, it always comes down to these three words: *do your job*.

This is the mantra of the New England Patriots, the team that has made it to the Super Bowl more times than any other team in the NFL.[5] It's more than just a battle cry. It's the foundation of the team's success. It's taught from day one, and the players know exactly what it means. Every single person on the team has a very specific set of tasks, and the only thing they need to worry about is executing those tasks to perfection. Do your job—not whatever you feel like, not someone else's job, not just part of your job. *Do your job*.

That's what I'm trying to teach you in this book. Doing your job means doing the six building blocks. Nothing else. You've spent your whole career distracted by other activities, and it's time to stop messing around and just do your job.

This isn't just about action. It's a shift in perspective: focus on the process and stop worrying about the result. When you worry,

5   And is tied for the most wins (6) with the Pittsburgh Steelers.

you are simply driving with the brakes on. Worry is not work. It just feels like work. Never lose sight of the fact that you have no control over the outcome, no control over who buys and who sells and when and how often. What you have control over is what you do every day.

Do your job.

Get better at it every day.

Agents get hung up on the result, so they chase after deals and rarely do what they're actually supposed to do. They all want to hedge their bets, do a little of this and a little of that, go a mile wide and an inch deep. Even when they think they know what their job is, most agents chase instead. Why?

The answer goes all the way back to Part I of this book. They don't understand the true nature of this business. They bounce back and forth between fear and hope—an exhausting place to exist. They are ruled by bad habits and false expectations. They haven't learned to be coachable. They want easy. They want now. They join the flavor of the month club, jumping from one new idea to the next. They fall for all the workshops and seminars that teach them how to chase, promising instant gratification.

This whole book is about avoiding that path—building relationships instead of chasing deals, having a long-term view of things instead of a "where is my next deal coming from" attention span. Your job as a real estate professional is outlined very specifically: focus on the six things that truly matter, and execute them consistently. There's no ambiguity. The market has nothing to do with what needs to be done every day. Your job is your job, and that doesn't change. Know what your job is, just do it, and again, get better at it.

Still, you'll be tempted to go off track. Your bad habits are strong; the groove is deep, they're embedded in your brain, and they don't want to die. This chapter will help you stay the course.

IT'S THIS . . . OR BURNOUT

I talk to agents every single day, and I can tell you one thing for sure. If they're not doing their job, they're on their way to burning out . . . or already there. I'm not talking about low-producing agents who only do a few deals a year. It's the top producers who are most at risk.

They sell millions and millions of dollars' worth of homes, reach the top of their markets, and then say to me: "I can't do this anymore. I'm tired. I don't want this." Most of the time, they just plow ahead, continuing to do the same things as always because they're too afraid of what they might lose from doing business differently or leaving real estate altogether. Then they're just doing it to soothe their own egos, with little or no joy and little or no challenge.

Burnout is very real, and it can last years. Don't think it can't happen to you, because it will. If you do enough business, it's inevitable. When you start out, you think, *If I could make $100,000 a year, I'd be thrilled.* Then you do, and your goal becomes $250,000 . . . then $500,000 . . . then $1 million, $5 million, $10 million.

If you keep hitting the mark, you'll find that no amount is enough. You're never thrilled. All you can think is, *What if I can't do it again?*

My coaching around goals and business planning has shifted dramatically in recent years. I used to preach the gospel when it came to goals. The bigger, the bolder, the better. The art of the impossible. 10X everything. Moon shots. You name it. I would have clients write detailed vision statements of what they wanted their life to be like and comprehensive plans to make it happen.

No more.

Today, I coach people to do their job, the six building blocks. Every day, the goal is the same: do your job, be present, serve the moment, elevate it, and most importantly . . . enjoy it.

When the goalpost keeps getting moved every year, when nothing is ever enough, when you are pitting your will against the will of the universe in an effort to achieve your goals, when the goal is ruling you and not the other way around . . . you are entering the danger zone. This kind of behavior is not sustainable. It always ends poorly. When you sell your soul for a shrinking percentage of market share or when you believe you are your ranking, it's not a good look.

Why do you really set goals in the first place?

This goes back to the false belief that getting more of what you want and avoiding what you don't want is the ticket to a great life. This thought process is a surefire recipe for suffering. If you want a better life, you can have it right now. Your ability to enjoy all of life does not have to be conditional on anything. You don't need to reach or exceed a goal to be happy. You can live in harmony with what is. You can choose unconditional happiness and practice nonresistance in this very moment. You don't need anything. There is nothing to fear. There are no "problems" in the outside world—only life.

I have watched too many top-performing clients stress themselves out over goals to the point where the only thing that mattered was whether they were reaching their goals or not. When you are selling over three hundred homes per year or over $500 million in closed sales volume and you are still worried about what comes next, something is very wrong with that picture.

I know you are reading this and saying to yourself, *If I ever get to those numbers, I am going to love my life!*

No, you won't. You'll still be chasing the next deal. You'll be worried the wheels are going to fall off the bus at any moment. You'll be looking over your shoulder at who is catching up to you.

Count on it. You will just keep moving the goal line on yourself. There is no answer to how much is enough.

That's because as your production increases, your goals become less about *having* enough and more about *being* enough. Your ego and identity get so wrapped up in your results that your goals mean more to you than the effort you give each day. That's when you're at risk of spinning out, and it's why my coaching around goals has shifted so dramatically. If your goal is all about force, pitting your will against the will of the universe, you are going to lose that battle.

It's not that more is inherently bad. It depends on how you get there. When you get to more by chasing, you burn out. When you do it by doing your job, you can keep going forever.

FOLLOW THE GUARDRAILS

The six building blocks are guardrails that keep you on the right path. The outside world and your survival mind are always trying to pull you off track. As I said in Chapter 1, every force imaginable is conspiring to make you into a commodity. Everybody wants you to chase. If you're not aware of this pull, you'll get swept into the current.

The path you're trying to stay on is the one that leads to a repeat and referral business that's sustainable, scalable, and maybe one day saleable. The only other alternatives—at least that I've seen—are stagnation or burnout. The building blocks are the only things that will protect you from those outcomes.

A Mindset of Harmony protects your mind. It frees you from the tyranny of your preferences so you can stop living every day in a state of fear or battle. It calms your inner turbulence so you can finally experience peace, even if the outside world is full of challenges. It enables you to get in alignment with the nature of the universe and this business so you can actually enjoy your work and your life.

Time blocking protects your time. It gives you control over your most precious asset so you can use it for the activities that will get the results you care about. It prevents you from falling prey to the demands and priorities of others who do not care about building your business. It shields you from the pretenders who aren't serious about working with you and only want to waste your time.

CRM protects your relationships. It holds you accountable for doing the work it takes to keep relationships alive. It makes it easy to do that work so you don't have to think or question—all you have to do is make calls. By nurturing those relationships, it fills your repeat and referral pipeline, positioning you as the Favorite for more and more people over time.

Process protects you from mistakes. It gives the client the smoothest experience possible, elevating their trust in and satisfaction with you. It eliminates the stress of mental to-do lists and constant firefighting. It builds equity in your business so it can continue generating value for you even after you retire.

Tactical Empathy protects you from convincing. It puts you in alignment with the way people actually make decisions—with emotion, not fact, logic, and reason. It allows you to advise and influence without pushing and persuading. It makes you the trusted advisor who puts your clients' interests first, above your own.

Managing your numbers protects your resources. It grounds you in the reality of how your business is actually doing instead of wishful thinking based on intuition. It prevents you from wasting time and money on activities that don't produce results. It keeps your spending aligned with your business strategy.

As I've said before, following these guardrails *will* make you uncomfortable at first. You're used to going all over the place at will, and staying within these six building blocks will feel restrictive. You'll want to break free and go back to the endless choices, distractions, and chaos because you'll be afraid you're missing out on something. But more choice doesn't solve anything. As David Brooks said, "The life well lived is a journey from open options to unwavering commitments."

If you make the commitment to stay within these boundaries, you'll find that your work becomes dramatically simpler and easier. There are *so many things* you don't need to do. Right now, those things take up a massive share of your time and energy. Put up these guardrails, and they disappear. You can just do these six things to the best of your ability every day, then go home and actually live your life.

YOU HAVE TO LET GO

At every level of growing your business, it comes down to letting go. You can't get to the next level by doing what you did before. At first, you let go of the administrative work by getting an assistant so you can focus on sales. Then, you let go of the buyers so you can focus on sellers. If you choose to build a team, eventually you let go of sellers to focus on strategic leadership.

This is the number one lesson by far and the hardest one to swallow. Fear of loss is the strongest motivator, at least twice as strong as desire for gain. So the more business you do, the harder it is to let go because the more you have to lose. The natural tendency is to hold on even harder, which consumes a tremendous amount of energy . . . until you burn out.

You think that if you don't hold on, it will disappear, but that's not true. What I've observed very clearly over the years is that there is *not* a direct correlation between effort and results in the short run. Everyone wants to believe there is, but there just isn't. Over and over, I see agents get wildly different results from one year to the next with the same level of effort. There are simply too many factors that are outside your control in this business.

The correlation between efforts and results happens over a much longer period of time. Again, as human beings, we tend to overestimate what we can get done in a year and underestimate what we can get done in a decade. When you stick to a single path and just take one small step after another, day after day, you *will* make progress—a lot more than if you're constantly jumping from one path to another in search of shortcuts.

So, I'm not saying don't do anything—I'm saying do your job. You may have an amazing year one year and not so much the next. That's just reality. You have to accept it. You can't change it, no matter how hard you try. You can only do the things that are within your control, and those are the six building blocks.

Letting go never ends, no matter how high you rise. One of my clients had built a huge team with massive production, in the hundreds of millions. Over the years, he had let go of almost everything—the admin work, the buyers, the sellers—but he was still burning out because he was clinging to one last thing: his ego. He was still trying to drive everything with personality, and because of it, his team was in chaos, despite their sparkling sales figures.

At that point, he had two choices: ride it into the ground or let go and rebuild the team from the inside out. Thankfully, he chose the latter. He admitted that he couldn't do it all himself, and he brought in a professional consultant to help build the systems and culture his team needed. Only by letting go of *everything*, including his ego, could he build a lasting business without destroying himself.

■ ■ ■

For most agents, the worst day of the year is January 1. That's when you look back at the past year and think, *Oh my God, I have to do this all over again.* If you just had your best year ever, you're wondering, *Can I do it again?* If you just had your worst year, the question is, *What if it happens again?*

Either way, you have a big pit in your stomach because you don't know why you got the results you got last year. You assume it must have been something you did because you've been taught that you're the one making things happen or not happen. But you don't know what it was, so you don't know how to change or replicate it. You feel like you're starting from scratch every year, which is why you're always looking for new ideas.

When you do your job, you're not starting from scratch. You're building a foundation of relationships, which keeps getting bigger and stronger every year. Then, January 1 is just another day. It's not a time to panic or set meaningless goals that you'll abandon within a month or two. Just like any other day, you go to work and do your job, knowing that you're focused on the only six things that matter in your business.

Know your job.

Do your job.

Get better at your job.

11: REAL ESTATE TEAMS

The idea that "more is better" leads down a very predictable path in real estate. First, you get great at selling. You sell so well that at some point, you start bringing in more business than you can handle by yourself. You think, *If I had more people, I could make more money.* So, you partner with another agent, or hire one.

This is the beginning of a very slippery slope.

In real estate, people think teams are a magic pill—a quick way to increase capacity and, therefore, income. In reality, they're the fastest way to work harder, make less money, and have more stress than before.

Here's what usually happens. The team expands organically in response to demand; the more business you can drum up, the more people you hire. The problem is, you've never been taught how to manage other people, let alone lead a team. You expected everyone to be as capable and dedicated as you, but they're just not. So, you spend all your time teaching them how to do their work, micromanaging it, or just doing it for them out of sheer necessity. It feels more like babysitting than leading.

Plus, you don't have a business plan, systems, or policies in place—who has time for that? You're too busy selling. So, everyone is doing things their own way, expectations and consequences are as clear as mud, and you have no idea whether any of this chaos is getting you the financial results you wanted.

Yikes. So much for that magic pill.

That said, teams *can* work in real estate. In fact, I think they're the future of real estate. High-performing teams are rare now, but in the next decade or so, I expect them to dominate many major markets.

That's the key term: *high-performing*. Today, most real estate "teams" aren't real teams at all, let alone high-performing ones. Building a great team is a completely different job from being a solo real estate agent, and very few team leaders understand that.

I wrote an entire book about this, with the help of my coauthors Dana Green and Jonathan Lack: *The Real Estate Team Playbook*. In this chapter, I'll give you a brief overview of the main takeaways from that book. To be honest, my primary goal is to scare you out of starting a team, especially if the idea is to make more money fast.

THREE TYPES OF TEAMS

When most agents think of starting a team, they picture a loose collection of individuals who use the same brand and share some resources but essentially take care of themselves. They imagine they'll be able to go on doing what they've been doing, but with a bunch of people around to take the clients they don't want. They'll take a generous split for providing leads and some basic support services, and that's that.

It's not that simple. In fact, that model is impossible to sustain. It's what the big brokerages have been trying to do for years, with steadily dwindling profit margins. They're all competing for the top producers, but those agents see little value in the brokerage;

everything it does, they're already doing better in-house. So, brokerages are forced to compete on price. The top split used to be 80 percent—now it's 95.

That cuts deep into the revenue needed to provide real value to the rest of the agents. So, it becomes a vicious cycle. The core business of big brokerages is running on a very tight margin, and what keeps them alive are the affiliate businesses—mortgage, title, and escrow. Your team won't have those extra revenue streams. You'll just wind up stuck in the same sinking ship, paying sky-high splits to keep the best agents while struggling to support the mediocre ones who actually need what you're trying to offer.

Bottom line: You have to provide value to your team. Otherwise, they'll end up costing you more than they bring in, and no business can survive that way.

There are three ways to provide that value—three fundamental team structures.

True Team

A true team is a tightly woven group of three to fifteen people focused on maximizing the production of the team as a whole, not as individuals.

This type of team is the most like the sports teams that were at the center of my life from childhood all the way through my four years with the Miami Dolphins. On a team, everyone has a role and responsibility, everyone is held accountable, and all the roles are interdependent. If you don't do your job, you're hurting everyone else. You win as a team, and you lose as a team.

This structure has massive potential for synergy. Because each person specializes in one area of the business, they become deeply skilled and highly efficient. Through close collaboration, the whole process of real estate becomes a perfectly tuned machine that delivers the best possible results and client experiences. This in turn fuels stronger loyalty in clients, which leads to higher repeat and referral rates. The whole is greater than the sum of its parts.

To build this kind of team, you have to give up your role as star player and become the head coach instead. You have to be the one to define the roles, hire the right people, train them, build a collaborative culture, set the strategy, and keep everyone aligned at all times. It's a full-time job, one that requires completely different skills from the ones you use as a solo agent.

That's where so many team leaders stumble in this process. They keep trying to play and never truly learn how to coach, so the team fails to become a cohesive whole, and the leader burns out trying to do everything at once. If you want the power of a true team where everyone collaborates for the good of the group, understand that it will require a major transformation on your part.

Mini Brokerage

In a mini brokerage, the goal is to create systems that help each agent maximize their individual production. This is the only model that works well for groups larger than about fifteen.

Unlike on a true team, agents in this type of organization are not highly interdependent. However, they still get significant value from being part of the team because the team provides resources, training, processes, and support that help them produce far more than they would on their own. Your job as team leader is to create all that value and help your agents reach their highest individual potential.

This allows you to scale up more than a true team can because close collaboration breaks down when there are too many people involved. It also leaves more room for you to continue handling some of your own deals—typically only the very high-value ones, since you need to allocate time for building systems and supporting your team. Another advantage of this model is that it tends to attract high performers who want more freedom and less hand-holding.

However, that independence can also be a pitfall. In this type of organization, it's usually more difficult to get agents to conform to team culture and ways of working. And because their roles aren't specialized, there is more competition within the team, which can create a toxic environment and high turnover.

The key to success with a mini brokerage is providing value that agents are willing to pay a meaningful split for—support that makes their lives easier and increases their productivity. That's the only way to make the brokerage model sustainably profitable.

Rainmaker Team

A rainmaker team is a group of three to ten people designed to maximize the production of the team leader.

If you don't want to give up your role as star seller, this is the team structure for you. Unlike a true team or mini brokerage, a rainmaker team revolves entirely around the leader. The purpose of every other team member is to maximize the time and attention you can devote to selling. If the team includes other agents, their role is to take the leads you don't have time for, not to go out and get leads for themselves.

This structure allows you to stay in your comfort zone. You can continue to focus on selling and not worry about transforming into a head coach or maximizing anyone else's production. You will still need to build some systems and train your team, but the leadership and management demands are relatively light.

This comes at a significant cost, which is that your ability to step away from the business is extremely limited. The other team structures allow you to work your way to a place where very little of the day-to-day business operations depends on you personally. This structure does not. You are the sales engine, and there is no one who can replace you. This means it's difficult, if not impossible, to take an extended break or to sell the business when you retire.

Still, a rainmaker team is probably the best option for most agents with team aspirations. Few agents are truly ready to take on the leadership roles that true teams and mini brokerages demand. However, many top-producing solo agents would benefit from having a strong support team that allows them to use their time and skills more effectively.

Regardless of which team structure you choose, there is power in a group of people working toward a shared goal. There is leverage, efficiency, and synergy. When everyone is in the same boat, rowing in the same direction, in sync with each other, they can go much farther and faster than if they were each in their own boats.

Already, a few top real estate teams are redefining the limits of production, taking their annual volume well into the hundreds of millions, even billions of dollars. But there are no shortcuts to this. Building a team is a long-term investment that requires serious commitment and a major change in your job description.

SELLING IS NOT LEADING

The reason most agents fail to build a thriving team is they don't understand the difference between selling and leading. Even if your boat is full of the best rowers, someone has to coordinate them, choose the destination, and keep the journey on track. Let's talk about what that work entails.

Setting strategy. This is even more crucial for a team than for an individual agent. You can't possibly get everyone rowing in the same direction if they don't understand what the destination is. As the team leader, it's up to you to define your competitive advantage and decide how to use and strengthen it. You also need to communicate this clearly to the team and build it into the guidelines and expectations that govern their work.

Creating culture. Your team doesn't have to agree on everything, but they do have to buy into a shared set of values that define who your team is and how you do business. How do you think, speak, and act? When it comes time to make tough decisions, what do you prioritize? Every person on your team will either contribute to this culture or undermine it. It's your job to choose people who fit the culture and hold them accountable for living it—which can be a real challenge, given the independent contractor mindset that pervades this business. You need people who have their hands up to contribute, not their hands out to receive. "Team First" is not a natural concept in real estate. You cannot overlook the importance of intentionally establishing this kind of chemistry between every member of your team.

Building processes. You learned about the importance of process in Chapter 7. In a team, it's even more crucial. Without comprehensive, robust processes, you're just bringing people into chaos. Everyone will do things their own way, causing endless problems for each other and the clients. As team leader, you must ensure that your processes are being continuously refined, particularly whenever a problem arises that could have been prevented.

Supporting people. As team leader, your job is no longer to sell homes—it's to help your team sell homes. They're the ones you want to see closing deals and getting thank-you notes, good reviews, and referrals. You'll need to spend significant time training and coaching them as well as informing them on the state of the market and the strategic message they should be communicating to clients.

Correcting course. You're the one with a bird's eye view of the business, the market, the competition, and your strategic goals. That's why one of your most important tasks is to keep everything aligned. That means assessing finances and other key metrics as well as team member performance. Sometimes, you'll have to make tough decisions about people and money that won't make everyone happy. It takes real discipline to follow your strategic model and not let feelings blow the business off course.

Managing money. You're responsible for keeping the business afloat and for ensuring that every member of the team does their part to support that outcome. There's no point in building a team just to grow the gross revenue; if your profits don't grow too, you're better off on your own. This is where so many team leaders falter. They don't realize how much their agents cost—usually $40–50K per year each, plus all the time and effort you spend on them (which you could have spent selling). Given that, each agent should generate *at least* $100K in revenue for you, which is only $50K in profit. If that's not happening, you need to look closely at your business model and your team members.

This is a *lot* of work—far too much for a star player to simply add onto their plate. If you try to do it all, you'll burn out faster than ever. That's the trap every team leader walks into. You have to pick one role or the other. Being the star player is what's natural . . . but then you have to hire a head coach, and no one wants to do that.

Either way, you have to let go—let go of your production or let go of running the show. If you can't let go, it won't work.

IT'S NOT ABOUT YOU

In the end, building a team is about far more than just hiring people. It's a wholesale shift in perspective, from "me" to "we." If you want to scale up your business while retaining your quality of life, well, you only win when your team wins. That means you have to build an organization designed to help other people succeed, not just you.

In fact, the better your team can function without you, the more valuable it is to you and potential buyers. If your team depends on you to constantly feed them leads and clean up their messes, you can never get away from the grind. In contrast, with a well-established, high-performing team, you can take a long vacation or even a sabbatical and trust that the business will continue to function while you're away.

Plus, at the end of your career, you'll find that all your hard work has built something that can continue to generate value for you even after you retire. For most agents, their last deal is their last paycheck. But for a team leader who has done their job well, the team itself has equity. It can be sold to a family member, an employee, or even a third-party buyer. But this only works if the team doesn't revolve around you—if another leader could take it over and continue producing similar results.

Don't fool yourself into thinking this will be quick or easy. Too many agents start teams with the fantasy that they'll attract other agents just like them, not have to invest anything in them, and make lots of money off of them. It doesn't work that way.

I should know—I've seen agents start teams and then disband them once they realize they're only running an adult day care center, managing other people's emotions and listening to their whining. One of my coaching clients built her team up to six agents, but despite the effort she poured into it, none of them were producing at a substantial level. She let them all go and kept only her assistant, and she now makes $1 million a year with a fraction of the headache.

Most agents, if they're honest with themselves, would do better as a solo agent with a small support team than as a true team leader. If you're a superstar seller, having one or two executive assistants and one or two support agents to take care of excess business would enable you to leverage your time a lot more effectively. The big difference is that this structure would never allow you to extract yourself from the business—it all revolves around you. That's okay, as long as you understand it and accept the limitations it creates.

■ ■ ■

Let's be honest: It's hard enough to get yourself to do the six building blocks. As a team leader, it will be your job to get *other* people to do them—and you can't teach people to do something you don't know how to do.

Are you prepared for that? That's what it takes to get everyone on the same boat rowing together. A team is about synergy and leverage, which can't exist when everyone is doing their own thing.

That said, a team doesn't have to have outrageously high production to be successful. If you can build a system where everyone can produce ten to fifteen deals a year, you've got something. Not everyone needs to sell one hundred homes and make $1 million a year. Some people just want a good job, with support, opportunity, structure, and social interaction. That's something a good team can provide that a brokerage can't.

If you're still seriously considering starting a team—or if you already have one—I strongly recommend you read *The Real Estate Team Playbook*. It's a much more in-depth resource on building a successful team, one that allows you to scale up your business without burning out, and possibly even sell it one day.

Just recently, after a session with a team leader I have been coaching for many years, I sent the following email to all the teams I currently coach. It's a perfect window into the problems teams struggle with every day. Every current and future team leader needs to read this very carefully and evaluate their team through this filter.

One thing has become abundantly clear to me in working with the numerous teams I work with . . .

STOP ALL THE ADULT DAY CARE!!
IMMEDIATELY!!
STOP INVESTING RESOURCES IN NONPRODUCTIVE PEOPLE!!

Time rarely makes the wrong things better. This is a performance business. The numbers don't lie. Don't let your team be a black hole that consumes your entire being.

In order for people to be productive (and that means at least ten to fifteen-plus deals per year), they must . . .

1. Have the right mindset/attitude
2. Have the right skillset
3. Give the right level of effort every week

Above everything, any team agent must be coachable. Being coachable means doing what you tell them to do. Not complicated.

The number one thing you get paid for as a real estate agent is consistency. You know this from your own experience in this business. No one gave you anything. You had to learn how to be successful by doing . . . and a lot of trial and error.

Any team agent can benefit from your journey. They don't need to make every mistake you made. You can accelerate their progress. HOWEVER, THEY MUST LISTEN AND DO WHAT YOU SAY!!

They don't need to put their own spin on anything. If any of your team members think they know better than you in terms of what it takes to be productive . . . LET THEM GO ASAP!!

Any team member must be prepared to show up and work at least fifty-plus hours every week. Nothing less. This is nonnegotiable.

And stop this ridiculous habit of filling in for team members because they have something else to do. They fill in for you . . . NOT THE OTHER WAY AROUND!!

Any team agent must be 100 percent proficient in CRM. This is mandatory.

Any team agent must be spending at least thirty minutes every day learning, studying, and role-playing.

If you are being honest with yourself . . . as team leader, you are spending the vast majority of your time trying to beg people to do the bare minimum required. This is a complete and total waste of your time. STOP IT!!

It doesn't take more than ninety days to figure out whether someone is going to succeed in this business. They either have the X factor or they don't. If you are not sure about someone . . . that probably means NO.

Your responsibility is to provide them with a structure that promotes success, and then you must hold them accountable to the process. No excuses and no stories.

Most team leaders hang on to the wrong people for too long and give their agents way too much rope. Being too nice and giving people the benefit of the doubt weakens your leadership ability. Don't keep people based on HOPE. When you keep nonproductive people on the team, it impacts all your productive people in a negative way. You will be much better served doubling down on the producers and letting go of everyone else.

TEAM is way harder than anyone realizes. You can't be both Rainmaker and Team Leader. You have to understand what role you are going to fill.

TEAM is a solid ten-year commitment. You have to get so many factors right: the systems, the people, the culture, the strategy, the money. All of it, or it doesn't work. There are so many dots to connect . . . including some that you are not even paying attention to.

The way most teams are set up right now leads to more work, less money, and more stress for you! Would I be wrong to think that was not your intention in building your team?

This is the year to strip everything down to the foundation, only keep what actually works, and grow from there.

YOU MUST GET RID OF ANY TRACE OF HOPE!!

HOPE IS A TEAM KILLER!!

12: BE A **FULL FEE** AGENT

There's one decision that affects your business more than any other. It affects how much money you take home. It affects how many years you need to work. It affects how your clients perceive you and how you serve them. In some way, it touches every aspect of your business.

It's your fee.

I define a full fee as 6 percent, with 3.5 percent going to the listing agent.[6] There are very few markets where it's still common practice to charge a full fee. If you listen to agents talk about it, a full fee sounds like an urban myth. There is an overwhelming belief industry-wide that you can't charge a full fee and thrive in this business. Almost every agent in the country is convinced that 6 percent is impossible, and they act like there is nothing they can do about it.

Let me be clear: this is completely, entirely, 100 percent false.

I have agents asking for and getting 6 percent every day. Every single one of them is doing it in a market where most agents are

---

6   There are a few markets where an even split between the buyer and seller side is required, but in most cases, 3.5 percent to the seller's agent and 2.5 percent to the buyer's is possible.

charging 5 or less. It doesn't matter. It *is* possible, for them and for you.

It's not just possible—it's necessary. This is not about greed. It's about choosing not to make yourself a commodity. It's about committing to a business based on relationships, not chasing. It's about holding yourself to a higher standard and letting go of anyone who asks you to lower it.

Building your business around charging a full fee is the smartest move you can make in real estate. When you do this, you can't be the cheapest, so you have to be the best. It puts the right kind of pressure squarely on you to discover what it means to work at your highest level. Your focus shifts from worry to work. Every day becomes an all-out pursuit of getting better in every way.

That's why your fee is the ultimate test of whether you're doing your job. There's no way to successfully charge a full fee without executing all six building blocks consistently. So, by choosing to charge 6 percent, you are holding yourself accountable for doing everything you've learned in this book. This is the number one way to put more money in your pocket *and* serve the best interests of your clients at the same time. These two things go hand in hand.

In fact—and I know I'll catch flak for this—if you're not charging a full fee, you're wasting your time. You'll work for ten, twenty, thirty-plus years and end up with your head barely above water. It's that important.

I readily concede that most agents don't charge 6 percent. Even top-producing agents don't—they'll openly admit that they choose market share over charging a full fee. They'll tell you that asking for 6 percent is a suicide mission.

Well, as Henry Ford said, "There are those who think they can and those who think they can't. They're both right."

If I've learned one thing from my thirty-plus years and 60,000+ hours of coaching real estate agents, it's that charging a full fee is the most effective way to build and grow your business . . . and the real reason no one gets 6 percent is because everyone is too afraid to ask for it. This is the aspect of your business that I'm most passionate about—so much that I wrote a whole book on it with Chris Voss, *The Full Fee Agent*. In this chapter, you'll learn why charging a full fee is so powerful and what it takes to do it successfully.

THERE'S ALWAYS A REASON

When I coach agents on this, I always meet a concrete wall of resistance a mile high. *I could never get away with asking for 6 percent,* they tell me. *No one in my market charges that much. Other people are successful without charging that much.*

You know what I hear hiding behind those objections? *I'm scared. What if it doesn't work? What if the client says no?*

It's all coming from a place of fear. And what do we do with fear? We examine it, then let it go. So, let's talk about what you're really afraid of: losing business.

Let me remind you of something you already know: Before you ever talk to a prospect, you are already the Favorite or the Fool. They already did their research and formed a strong opinion. The decision is 80 percent made before they pick up the phone, and it's not based on fact, logic, or reason. It's an emotional choice. What matters most is not price but trust—who do they trust to put their interests first when handling their biggest asset?

Your commission does not win or lose you business. If you're the Favorite, they'll pay what you ask. If you're not, they won't—but they were never going to go with you anyway. If your commission is a dealbreaker, that's the clearest possible sign that you're not the Favorite.

So, will you lose out on some deals that you might otherwise have gotten? Yes, but not nearly as many as you think. At least 80 percent of the time, people hire the Favorite no matter how hard the Fools chase them with discounts and perks. So at most, you might lose 10 to 20 percent of the deals you currently get—the ones where you were the Fool but got hired anyway because you sold a little piece of your soul.

Still, you come out ahead. The difference between 2.5 percent and 3.5 percent is a whopping 40 percent. There is *no way* you'll lose 40 percent of your business because you charge a full fee. The more repeat and referral business you do, the safer you are; those clients care far more about the trust in your relationship than your fee.

When it comes to discounting, the worst offenders are the top agents. They've amassed big market share, and they're terrified to lose it because it feeds their ego, not to mention their marketing claims. Market share becomes more important than anything else—more than client experience, quality of life, and even profits. So, they continue selling their souls and making themselves into commodities, charging 5 percent, or 4, or even less.

Here is a real-life example. Pay close attention—you'll recognize this challenge.

A top agent ($100 million producer) was invited to give a listing presentation. She was in competition with two other top agents, including her main competitor. She put in hours of prep time, adding every bell and whistle she could. The actual presentation was over two hours, and she felt very confident in how it was received. She sent a long follow-up email right after the appointment but did not get an immediate response, which triggered some old battle wounds.

When she finally heard back, it was a request for more information, which she willingly provided. Silence again. Then, another request for an in-person meeting to review some specific pricing data. After the second meeting, the agent was beginning to think she was the Fool in the game. In fact, she was quite sure of it, which triggered more inner turmoil.

Then, surprisingly, after being on pins and needles for over ten days, she learned the business was hers . . . with one small catch. She needed to work for a 1.5 percent commission on her side of the deal (4 percent total). It was either that or lose the deal to the other agent. She agreed to work for the reduced fee.

The agent felt this was a hard-earned victory, and most every agent would agree. But was it?

The seller did a masterful job of getting three top agents to share all their information for free. They pitted all the agents against each other, and they worked their top choice down to a 1.5 percent commission. Did the agent really win? Maybe, maybe not. There is no way there won't be some resentment on the agent's part, as much as she would deny it.

Here's what I want you to think about. When you get to the point in your career where you are experienced, have a reputation as a top producer, and work your butt off for your clients . . . do you still want to have to give your money away to get business? It is a fair question that needs to be asked and answered.

By the way, there is another little twist to this story. Less than two months earlier, this same agent was in a similar situation. Again, she discounted her fee to get a listing she really wanted. At that time, she swore she would never do it again. And this is an agent whose standard is 5 percent, not 6.

WARNING: discounting your fee to get business is an extremely hard habit to break. On one deal, it doesn't seem like a big sacrifice . . . but it never ends up being just one deal.

Tell me, in what other business do the best professionals charge the least? It makes no sense. In fact, I'd argue that anyone giving their money away to get business isn't a top performer at all. That takes no skill whatsoever. You know what does? Charging a full fee.

All this insanity stems from fear of loss. The moment you tell yourself that something is better than nothing, you've started down this dangerous path. You will always be able to come up with a "legitimate" reason to give your money away, to let someone else reach into your pocket. But as soon as you start to compromise your standards on price, you're compromising your entire business.

YOUR FEE DICTATES YOUR QUALITY

A Ford will get you to the same place a Rolls Royce will. The difference is in the experience. It's economy versus first class, fast food versus fine dining, discount fashion versus couture. The two things perform the same basic function, but some people want to pay more for a better experience.

The truth is, those people are better clients than discount shoppers. They're choosing you because they actually want you, not because you're the cheapest. They believe in your competence and trustworthiness, so they'll be open with you, collaborate, and take your advice.

In contrast, discount shoppers are looking to squeeze the most out of you for the least money—in other words, to turn you into a commodity. They won't trust you to protect their interests, and why should they? You're the cheapest, not the best. So, they'll doubt and resist you the whole way, eating up your time and causing stress. Plus, there's no appreciation for the discounted fee or any other concessions you make. There's only an expectation. They feel entitled to reach into your pocket.

Every bad client takes up the space of two good clients. They demand more attention, cause more conflict, and create more problems for you to resolve. They want to make sure they get their money's worth, so they're more controlling and involved, which only makes it harder to do your job.

Working with full fee clients is a much better experience all around. When there's a real relationship based on trust, you can be so much more efficient and effective, with far less stress. However, until you make 6 percent your standard, you'll never know what a difference this makes.

Again, charging a full fee also makes you a better agent. If you're going to price yourself as the high-quality option, you have to elevate your game to fulfill that promise. You need to be more knowledgeable in every aspect of the business: local inventory and home values, home prep and marketing, negotiations, contract language, client service, and everything in between. You also need to be more skilled at building relationships and playing the role of the trusted advisor.

This doesn't mean you must work *more*—just smarter and more consciously. In other words, you have to stop messing around and focus on the six building blocks. Do your job. That's the work that will elevate your quality and justify a full fee. It's also the work that will build relationships so that you're the Favorite, and your fee is the last thing your clients are worried about.

I can't overstate the degree to which this one decision drives everything in your business. One of my long-time coaching clients has built her business up to two-hundred-plus deals a year. From the outside, everything looks perfect. She has the production, rankings, market share, brand recognition, the works. She's a smart, honest, kind person. Any agent would want to be her, and any client would want to hire her . . . but she lives in a perpetual state of burnout.

She made just one critical mistake: she convinced herself she couldn't maintain 6 percent as her standard.

She started at 5 percent, worked her way to 6, and held that as a standard for many years. Over time, she increased her market share dramatically. Then one day, another agent got very aggressive and started nipping at her heels. She hit the panic button and convinced herself she could no longer charge a full fee. Going from 3.5 percent to 2.5 percent on her side really ate at her profit margin. From that point, it became harder and harder to enjoy what she was doing.

When 6 is your standard, everything is simple. If they don't pay it, they're not your client, and you're okay either way. If for every deal you have to decide whether to discount and how much, that's unbelievably stressful. Just imagine running a shop: if you have to haggle over every sale, your job is a lot harder than if customers simply choose to pay the sticker price or not.

This stress bleeds into every part of your life. It feels like everyone is tugging on you all the time. That's why this agent started burning out about four years ago and has never been able to recover.

DO THE MATH

I can't talk you into charging a full fee. You have to decide it's important to you. Just know that this decision will impact your entire career, so you should understand the consequences. If you choose not to do this, you're choosing to work harder and make less—a *lot* less. And you are unintentionally pushing your retirement down the road by years.

If you actually do the math, when you charge 2.5 percent or less on the listing side, you're basically running a break-even business. Between the transaction expenses and your overhead, there are a lot of costs to cover, and they can easily eat up most of your commission. At best, you'll end up a little ahead . . . and sometimes a little behind.

Now, here's a scarier calculation. Go back over the last twelve months and add up all the money you gave away: all the discounts and rebates, all the costs that shouldn't have been yours, everything you "contributed" to make a deal go together. What would you have made if you had charged a full fee on every deal with no financial concessions?

You will be astonished. What you're giving away isn't just your profits—it's your retirement! At 2.5 percent instead of 3.5, you'll be working five to ten years longer and looking at a very different quality of life in your golden years.

I just had a client go through this exercise. Over the past four years or so, she has taken 107 listings (all by Zoom, in case you were interested). At least 90 percent of these listings were at 6 percent, keeping 3.5 percent. The only time she doesn't get 6 percent is when she has to co-list with someone who is not so brave. Her average list price is $1.7 million. If you do the math, getting 6 percent and keeping 3.5 percent instead of 2.5 percent put an additional $1.8 million in her pocket. And this is just over four years—imagine what this number looks like over thirty years.

Again, when you look at it one deal at a time, it doesn't seem so bad. So what if you have to give away a few thousand dollars to get a commission? It's just the cost of doing business, right?

But it's never just one deal. Every time you do it, you set a precedent, not just for that client but for every person they ever refer to you. You're digging yourself into a very deep hole, one "little" discount at a time.

Here's another real-life example for you. An agent I coach was talking to the seller of a $4 million home. The seller was ready to list with the agent's top competitor but said she would change her mind if the agent agreed to a 4 percent commission.

The agent thought (like you would), *I want to break into this price point . . . it's me or my top competitor . . . the property will sell . . . I'll get to earn another commission when the seller buys . . . I would be stupid to turn this opportunity down.* In fact, all the agents in her mastermind group said it was a no-brainer. So, she did it, and the property sold in just two weeks.

It seems like a smart business decision. It always does at the time. But what happens now? What commission will that client expect next time? What will they tell their friends about this agent? Will she be able to charge a full fee with the next big client, or will she find another "legitimate" reason to give her money away?

This is why I said it's a slippery slope. It seems harmless at first, even smart. You tell yourself it's just this one time . . . but it's not. It never is. When you believe something is better than nothing, it always will be, and that's how this becomes a habit. That's how you give your retirement away.

Is that what you want to do? Give your money away to work more years serving clients who see you as a commodity? Why do that when you can keep your money to work with clients who trust you and value your work?

The funny thing is, the top agents who work with the highest-value homes are the most likely to give steep discounts. They justify it by saying their margins can afford it—after all, the expenses for selling a $20 million home aren't much different from those of a $10 million home. It's only fair that the client should expect a lower fee, agents tell themselves.

Wrong. Those clients are the exact people who voluntarily choose to pay more for everything in life—homes, cars, clothes, food, travel, *everything*. They want the best service, and they're willing to pay for it.

Again, there's always a reason to discount, but in the end, making that choice only shows that you don't think the value you provide is worth a full fee.

THE COMMISSION CONVERSATION

The commission conversation is by far the one that agents dread above all others. For most agents, the approach is to avoid it at all costs, hope the prospect never brings it up, and just slide it into the contract with no discussion whatsoever. If that doesn't work, plan B is to use facts, logic, and reason to convince the prospect of their value. If that's still not enough, plan C is to sell a little piece of their soul—offer discounts or other concessions until the prospect gives in.

No more of that. To charge a full fee, you need a different approach. As you learned in building block #5, use Tactical Empathy to get the elephants out early. Tackle the uncomfortable conversation as soon as possible.

Your first chance is on the pre-appointment video call. Bring it up in that first conversation.

Agent: I'm going to get something out on the table that might be a potential sticking point.

Seller: What's that?

Agent: My fee. I am a full service, full fee agent. I charge 6 percent, keeping 3.5 percent on my side and paying the agent representing the buyer 2.5 percent.

Seller: That is more than we expected.

Agent: This is my standard fee. It is the fee I charge everyone (. . . including my mother).

(If you are the Favorite, you have just given them enough reason to say okay. If you are the Fool in the game, they are probably going to push back harder.)

Seller: I can appreciate that, but all the other agents we spoke with were willing to work for less.

Agent: Most agents will work for less.

Seller: Is there any flexibility in your fee?

Agent: Sounds like my fee might be a dealbreaker for you.

Seller: Possibly.

Agent: If you truly believe in your heart of hearts that you can get the same result or better working with someone who charges less, that is probably the right move for you.

If you are the Favorite, they will pay you. If you are the Fool, they are going to try and make you wrong. Either way, you are demonstrating your skill, confidence, and ability to walk away gracefully. You're showing that you're not afraid to have a hard conversation. You're standing up for your interests the same way you'll stand up for theirs. Whether they say yes or no, you win. Standing firm on your fee is empowering; giving in is a hollow victory at best.

Remember, you're never trying to *convince* anyone of anything. You win or lose business because you're the Favorite or the Fool, not because you explain your value. If you're the Favorite, they'll pay your fee.

If they push back, listen closely. There are two kinds of objections. When you're the Favorite, they'll push back to make sure they're not leaving money on the table. They're just checking that you'll hold firm. Remind them of the real issue at hand:

"There's one question you have to ask yourself: how can you expect someone to stand up for you when they can't stand up for themselves?"

When you're the Fool, they'll try to make you wrong and put you on the defensive. They'll ask you to justify yourself and explain the extra value they'll get from paying you more. That's a clear sign that they don't see your value anyway, and they never will. Don't try to convince them—that's impossible. Just exit gracefully.

For this to work, you have to be willing to walk away. It goes back to building block #1: *let go*. Choose trust over fear. There will be other opportunities.

Any time commission comes up, put your Tactical Empathy to work. Use it to reframe the question for the client from one of money to one of trust.

For example, one night I got a panicked phone call from a long-term coaching client. She had just double-ended a $70 million deal. (Let that sink in.) Now, the client was coming back to her to ask for 1 percent back—$700,000. She didn't know what to do.

I suggested the following dialogue:

Agent: I am incredibly sorry, and I must apologize to you profusely.
Seller: Why?
Agent: I have done an absolutely horrible job for you. You must think the worst of me.
Seller: What are you talking about? You did an amazing job.
Agent: The fact that you are asking for 1 percent back tells me I must have really let you down and this is my punishment.
Seller: Never mind.

Guess what? It worked. The agent never thought she could muster the courage to say those words, but she did . . . and she kept $700,000 in her pocket.

■ ■ ■

No one else will tell you to charge a full fee. In fact, everyone else will tell you you can't do it. You have to decide who is right.

Just know that this isn't lip service—it's a call to arms. The difference between 3.5 and 2.5 is *profit*. You can't build a business if you spend more than you bring in, and no amount of wishful thinking will change that.

The truth is, most top agents work too hard and provide too much value to be discounting their fee. If you choose to continue doing this, know that you are choosing to work harder and longer for less—and you're also choosing to run a lower-quality business. You cannot be the best if you're the cheapest. Life doesn't work that way.

If you want to become a better real estate professional, charge a full fee. If you want to prioritize profit, client experience, and quality of life over market share, charge a full fee. If you want to retire comfortably at a reasonable age, charge a full fee.

That said, it's your money. You decide what to do with it, not me. I can only tell you how to get 6 percent and what that will do for you and your business. I can tell you that if you don't, you're not going to end up in a good place. Don't live in hope that it's all going to be okay somehow, because it's not.

Ultimately, it's your call.

Remember, the only obstacle to doing this is your own fear of losing business. But as you just learned, that fear is unfounded. You do not win or lose business based on your commission. You win or lose business because you're the Favorite or the Fool, and that's an emotional decision that takes place before the client even knows your fee.

At worst, you'll lose the deals you never should have won anyway—the ones you used to get by selling a little piece of your soul.

When you stop chasing the discount shoppers, you make room for the people you want to work with, and who want to work with you. And to live up to the promise of your price, you have to focus on doing your job—the six building blocks—to the absolute best of your ability every single day.

This transforms your business completely. The moment you start charging a full fee, everything changes for the better. And when you truly understand why people will pay you 6 percent and why they won't, making the full fee your standard will not seem as nearly daunting.

CONCLUSION

As I've said before, in real estate, you only learn by doing. The good news is, real estate is not rocket science. Hopefully, after reading this book, you will absolutely know the answer to the question, "What am I supposed to do?"

Everyone who gets into this business starts at ground zero. It is only through trial and error that you begin to figure things out. As you set out on this journey, you are going to make mistakes. You are going to encounter disappointment. You are going to experience frustration. Things will never go as quickly as you want. You will have to deal with rejection all along the way, and the rejections will sting and feel very personal (even though they are never personal and always temporary).

If you are not failing often, it is only because you are not trying. That's why I've said over and over that you must get comfortable being uncomfortable.

You are not the center of the universe. Be very clear on that. Just because you want something to happen means nothing. What you desire is irrelevant. You will go through tough times and down years. There will be stretches in this business when it seems like everyone and everything is against you.

This is a good thing. Being battle-tested in life is a positive. There is nothing wrong with a few scars and bruises to keep you humble. When you are in that moment, and you feel your back up against the wall, and your mind is trying to convince you that the end is near and you can't go on . . . these are the moments that change your life for the better.

For me, those moments include . . .

The fourth-grade piano recital where I froze up on stage and the All-Star Little League game where, as a pitcher, I got pummeled by the opposing team. In each case, I gave in to the pressure of the situation, and it got the best of me.

In my rookie year with the Miami Dolphins, I was walking out to the practice field before the sixth game of the year when Don Shula turned to me and said, "Son, you are not doing what we put you on this team to do." He then turned and walked away. Instead of freaking out, somehow I managed to gather my thoughts and made a very conscious decision: I would stop worrying about the outcome of the game and just give my absolute best effort. If that was good enough, great. If it wasn't good enough, I would still be okay. In that split second, I fully internalized what it means to not be attached to the outcome. This lesson has served me well.

On my first day on the government desk at Salomon Brothers, one of the accounts given to me wanted to make the "new kid" look good and gave me a billion-dollar trade to execute. That trade did not happen, and as I slinked back down into my seat, I realized I had no idea what I was doing. Not a clue. This was not a place where you get by "winging it." That light bulb moment was my catalyst to get up to speed and get my act together as quickly as possible.

After getting fired for the third time in my professional life by a startup real estate tech company in Seattle, I moved back to Santa Monica with no money, no clients, no momentum, and bills stacking up. As I sat in my living room, staring out the window, I had another light bulb moment of clarity: *I cannot afford my fear*. In that instant, I became 100 percent energized and focused, and I went to work doing what needed to be done.

Finally . . .

When the pandemic hit, I knew right away that no one was going to pay for coaching. I stepped back, analyzed the situation carefully, and came up with an idea for keeping people engaged in the coaching process in a frictionless way. In short, I made an offer that agents could not refuse. I launched that idea in two seconds flat, and my business skyrocketed from there.

These are the moments when life cuts through you like a knife, and you find out who you are and what your insides are made of. We have all been there. No one gets to breeze through life without coming face to face with their deepest fears and demons.

I know you can relate. Think back. What were your moments? What have been your "wake up" calls in life? What did you learn each time? How did they change the trajectory of your life? I love these moments. So many emotions come rushing to the surface all at once. Your entire state of being is transformed. You feel so alive when everything is on the line.

In *The Obstacle Is the Way*, Ryan Holiday states, "Nobody is born with a steel backbone. You have to forge it yourself. This thing standing in your way is not going anywhere. You're not going to out-think it or out-create it with some world-changing epiphany."

There is nothing you cannot endure and no situation you cannot overcome. No matter the obstacle, you will get through it. This too shall pass. Curiosity over anxiety. When you break it down and understand it, fear is your friend.

Ultimately, your job is to always be ready—ready to serve when the moment is ready, when all the factors outside your control get into alignment. This is what the six building blocks are all about.

Real estate looks easy from the outside, but once you're "in the arena," helping people buy and sell, it doesn't feel that way. You will have to learn to play under pressure. Every insecurity you have will be tested repeatedly. You are going to be an absolute mess at times. Welcome to the club.

Conversely, you will have unlimited opportunities to grow and challenge yourself to be the best possible version of you. Again, what doesn't kill you makes you stronger. Behind every mountain is another mountain. No one can get in your way in this business. No one is doing it *to* you. You are the only one who can put limits on yourself. This is a blue-sky business—opportunity is truly everywhere. You are surrounded by it at all times.

To use an old football expression, keep your head on a swivel. Eyes wide open, alert, awake, and alive. If you are not living on the edge, you are taking up too much space. As I tell my clients all the time, there is never a lack of opportunity, only a lack of awareness and effort.

Top performers in real estate are no different than top performers in every other profession. They share something in common: an all-out obsession with being great. "Greatness" might seem like a mysterious concept, but if you look closely, there's no mystery at all.

People who achieve greatness know exactly what they want to accomplish. They are single-minded in their purpose and believe 100 percent in their ability to achieve it. There is no room for doubt or worry. They commit themselves fully and say *no* to everything else.

They are open to new ideas and always seeking to learn and grow. They prepare themselves in every way possible, through study, training, practice, repetition, and conditioning. Every day is a relentless pursuit to get better. Their internal standards and expectations of themselves are simply higher than everyone else's.

They are always seeking some type of competitive advantage. No stone goes unturned.

They consciously install the right habits. They don't wing it or leave things to chance. Routine, strategy, and calculation are critical to their process. At the same time, they think on their feet and can improvise when the situation dictates.

They are intensely focused on their mission, tuning out all the noise and distraction that we all face in life. They outwork and outhustle everyone. They don't look for shortcuts or make excuses. They never let themselves off the hook. They understand the consequences of their actions and take full responsibility for what they do and don't do.

They take extreme care of themselves physically, mentally, emotionally, and spiritually. And yet, they make great sacrifices knowingly and willingly, and they play through the pain when necessary. They are meticulous when it comes to being ready. No detail is too small.

They seek coaching and feedback. They are truly self-aware and brutally honest with themselves. They are quick to adjust when necessary.

They test and challenge their limits at every opportunity, choosing bold action over safety. They thrive under extreme pressure and relax into it. They are resilient and bounce back quickly from defeat, more determined and resolute than ever.

They play with joy and love in their heart. They keep things in perspective and know how to pace themselves. Their attitude and effort elevate everyone around them. They know they cannot achieve what they want without the help of others.

They take nothing for granted. Everything must be earned. They understand the history of their game and want to be part of that history. They respect their profession and relish the challenge of being the very best they can be.

Bottom line: top performers are actively working toward greatness . . . *all the time.*

Now ask yourself: Are you the person I described above? Why or why not? We all have the ability to be great. Whether we exercise that ability or not is a choice. What choice are you making in your life?

At the end of last year, I got an email from one of my coaching clients. He said he had just had his best year in terms of personal income: $875,000 with only twenty-two closings. His previous record was $850,000 . . . but with forty-nine closings. He made more money with less than half the work because on every single one of those twenty-two deals, he charged 6 percent and kept 3.5. Even more importantly, he did it with *zero stress.*

This is what happens when you stop searching for new ideas and focus on executing the six building blocks you've learned in this book. None of them are complex or technically difficult. Real estate is not rocket science.

What makes the building blocks hard is that you've spent so many years doing the opposite. From your first day in real estate, everyone taught you to go out and make things happen, to chase, to make yourself into a commodity. No one taught you how this business really works. No one taught you to build long-term relationships.

Now, the greatest challenge is letting go of everything you used to do and believe so you can get in alignment with reality. Your survival mind will try to hold you back. It will tell you that the devil you know is better than the devil you don't know. It will come up with a thousand reasons to be afraid of trying something new.

But remember, the wisdom in this book comes from over 60,000 hours of coaching real estate agents. I know how hard you work. I know no one really understands or appreciates what you do. I know you don't need hype or false promises—just reality.

Given this is a blue-sky business and you are the only one who can get in your way, the question becomes: What are you willing to settle for? Most people settle for far less than what's possible, and they don't even realize they're selling themselves short.

You can do the same amount of business in less than half the time, or double your business. You can eliminate your stress and actually enjoy your work. You can have thirty-plus years of success, and maybe even sell your business at the end of it.

The only way to achieve all that is to commit to the six building blocks. Yes, they're the six things you least want to do . . . but they're also the only six things you really need to do.

Most agents will not do them. However, you are not most agents. You are you. And the question is, will *you* do them?

This makes me laugh a little. Could you imagine me as a young NFL rookie or even a seasoned veteran going up to Coach Shula and saying, "Don, I really like what you have to say. You make some great points. However, at this point in time, I think I will keep doing what I have always done." We all know what his reaction would have been!

Still, that's what most agents will do. The craving for what's easy, fun, interesting, instant, comfortable, and certain is that strong. It feels much nicer to think that you can make things happen, that you can do something today to get business tomorrow, that if you just keep chasing deals, you'll get where you want to go. There's a massive audience for that BS.

There's a much smaller audience for the truth. You can't make things happen—you have no control over most of the factors that affect your results. There is nothing you can do today to get business tomorrow—real estate is a relationship business, and relationships are a long-term game. No matter how hard you chase, you'll never get anywhere because you're running on a treadmill.

Most people don't want to work harder and make less, but until you step off that treadmill, that's the decision you're making. The point of this book is to wake you up to that choice. If you don't make a conscious, courageous commitment to the six building blocks, you'll keep doing what you've always done, hoping and praying you get a better result. That's the classic definition of insanity.

At the beginning of this book, I promised you would learn three things: (1) how to be coachable, (2) how to grow a repeat and referral business, and (3) how to enjoy every day no matter what.

Only a relentless focus on the six building blocks will make those things happen. I've seen it over and over: no one who is chasing is happy. More does not lead to happiness. It leads to a tighter and tighter death grip on your business, and the harder you hold on, the faster you burn out.

You have to let go. Let go of the fears that hold you back from doing what's necessary. Let go of the preferences that hold you hostage to a lifetime of suffering. Let go of your fantasies about how things should be and embrace what is. Let go of your goals and focus on the process.

This is what will change everything. For my coaching clients who have committed to this path, the quality of their business has exploded. They don't work 24/7 or exist in a perpetual state of fight or flight. They have stronger relationships with their clients and enjoy working with them. And because they've stopped wasting so much time, there's actually room to grow their business without sacrificing their personal lives.

That's what I want for you: to do well *and* be well. That's why I wrote this book.

Now, I've laid out the facts for you, and I've shown you the path forward, but I can't walk it for you. I can't do your job for you, and I can't make you do it. It's all up to you.

To borrow from coach Tony D'Amato (played by Al Pacino) in *Any Given Sunday*, you're in hell right now, believe me. You can stay there and get the shit kicked out of you, or you can fight your way back into the light. You can climb out of hell one inch at a time . . . by doing your job.

The choice is yours. Are you going to keep doing what you've been doing and continue to suffer and struggle, or will you do your job and build a business that allows you to thrive? Make that decision with the full knowledge of what's possible and what the consequences will be.

Chasing is a one-dimensional strategy in search of instant gratification. It is not focused, it is not efficient, and it does not build toward anything. It leads to a chaotic, hand-to-mouth existence. Every time you catch a deal, you experience a moment of relief from the chase, but as soon as that deal is done, you're back at square one. Because of that, most veteran agents don't have many years of experience—they have one year of experience repeated again and again. They're not getting better over time. They're just burning out.

The six building blocks are a multidimensional strategy. All the dots are interconnected: mind, time, people, process, skill, and knowledge. When you leverage them all together, you realize your full potential as a real estate agent. You build a foundation that gets stronger over time, so each successive deal becomes easier to get and easier to execute. The result is a business that can last for decades and support the life you always dreamed of living.

If you choose this path, you're probably going to need support. It's a very, very rare person who has the discipline to take on a change of this magnitude and see it through by themselves. As an author, I can teach you what to do. As a coach, I can hold you accountable for doing it and steer you back on track when you stumble. Together, we can accelerate your transformation, so you can reap the benefits sooner rather than later.

With or without a live coach, your next steps are clear.

Let go of your preferences and live in harmony.

Take control of your time and do what is most important.

Nurture your relationships.

Refine your processes.

Master Tactical Empathy.

Track and know your numbers.

Above all . . .

Do your job. It's not rocket science.

Printed in the USA
CPSIA information can be obtained
at www.ICGtesting.com
LVHW041931101123
763491LV00032B/1610/J